About Island Press

Island Press is the only nonprofit organization in the United States whose principal purpose is the publication of books on environmental issues and natural resource management. We provide solutions-oriented information to professionals, public officials, business and community leaders, and concerned citizens who are shaping responses to environmental problems.

In 2005, Island Press celebrates its twenty-first anniversary as the leading provider of timely and practical books that take a multidisciplinary approach to critical environmental concerns. Our growing list of titles reflects our commitment to bringing the best of an expanding body of literature to the environmental community throughout North America and the world.

Support for Island Press is provided by the Agua Fund, The Geraldine R. Dodge Foundation, Doris Duke Charitable Foundation, Ford Foundation, The George Gund Foundation, The William and Flora Hewlett Foundation, Kendeda Sustainability Fund of the Tides Foundation, The Henry Luce Foundation, The John D. and Catherine T. MacArthur Foundation, The Andrew W. Mellon Foundation, The Curtis and Edith Munson Foundation, The New-Land Foundation, The New York Community Trust, Oak Foundation, The Overbrook Foundation, The David and Lucile Packard Foundation, The Winslow Foundation, and other generous donors.

The opinions expressed in this book are those of the author(s) and do not necessarily reflect the views of these foundations.

The Last Refuge

David W. Orr

The Last Refuge

Patriotism,

Politics, and

the Environment

in an Age of Terror

ISLANDPRESS

Washington · Covelo · London

First Island Press cloth edition, March 2004
First Island Press paperback edition, August 2005

Library of Congress Cataloging-in-Publication data.

Orr, David W., 1944–
  The last refuge : patriotism, politics, and the environment in an age of
terror / David W. Orr.
      p. cm.
  Includes bibliographical references and index.
  ISBN 1-59726-032-0 (pbk. : alk. paper)
1. Political culture—United States. 2. Social values—United States.
3. Sustainable development—United States. 4. United States—
Politics and government—2001– I. Title.
  JK1764.O77   2005
  302.6'0973'090511—dc22   2005014648

British Cataloguing-in-Publication data available.

Design by Teresa Bonner
Text font: Miller Roman by Matthew Carter/The Font Bureau Inc.

Printed on recycled, acid-free paper

Manufactured in the United States of America
10 9 8 7 6 5 4 3 2 1

To Vaclav Havel, Nelson Mandela, and Paul Wellstone
Pioneers of twenty-first-century politics

Patriotism is the last refuge of a scoundrel.
    —Samuel Johnson

Necessity is the plea for every infringement of human freedom: it is the argument of tyrants; it is the creed of slaves.
    —William Pitt

Genuine politics—politics worthy of the name—is simply a matter of serving those around us: serving the community, and serving those who will come after us. Its deepest roots are moral because it is a responsibility expressed through action, to and for the whole. . . .
    —Vaclav Havel

Contents

Politics

Challenges

Reconstruction

Acknowledgments

Many of the chapters here first appeared in the journal *Conservation Biology* and owe a great deal to the thoughtful editorial comments and support of the editor, Gary Meffe. "The Education of Power" originated in part from collaboration with Hunter Lovins and a group organized in part by Ray Anderson that aimed to improve environmental policies of the current administration. Their willingness to reprint sections of our report is gratefully acknowledged. I acknowledge, too, permission to reprint previously published material from *Conservation Biology* and the University of Kentucky Press with appreciation. Finally, I appreciate the encouragement and editorial skill of Todd Baldwin at Island Press, without which this would have been a more tedious enterprise for author and reader alike.

Introduction to the 2005 Edition

I'll begin at the end of this short book and say that I want to take you to what Thomas Berry calls "the Great Work"—a call to national renewal that crosses the divisions between red and blue America.[1] In fact, I don't believe that we are nearly as divided between liberal and conservative as is often said. The great majority of us are a bit of both depending on the particular issue, and we change our minds over time as our perspectives change and we mature and grow wiser. At our best Americans are a pragmatic people, not ideologues. American history, our national shortcomings notwithstanding, is a noble chapter in the human story and I do not believe that it is nearly ended.

The United States was born in the revolutionary idea that all of us stand equally before the law—still a revolutionary idea. We came to believe that government ought to be of the people, by the people, and for the people—democratic, open, and accountable. In revolution we forged a country that became a nation through the tragedy of a civil war. We built continental prosperity, fought and beat the forces of tyranny in the twentieth century, and put men on the moon. But now virtually everyone across the spectrum of political opinions and religious persuasions agrees that we are in serious trouble. Some attribute this to the threat of terrorism and the hostility of Islamic fundamentalists. Some believe that the crisis is that of a decadent culture that needs spiritual renewal and more discipline. Some believe that we are in crisis because we are living far beyond our ecological and economic means. Less philosophically, most Americans experience one crisis or another in the daily effort to support a family and raise decent children in difficult economic circumstances and in confusing times. But most agree that something has gone seriously wrong in America.

The Great Work that Thomas Berry describes is not a political agenda, although it will eventually require solutions forged in the political arena. It begins, rather, with the call of duty and necessity that is thrust on societies by circumstance and fate at particularly perilous times in history. No generation ever chooses its great work. The young Americans that rose to the challenge of the Revolution or those called to battle in the Civil War did not choose those trials, yet they responded to them with courage and fortitude. Against the challenges of history, whatever they might be, the generation on trial is measured by its discernment, foresight, fairness, ingenuity, and magnanimity in its particular hour. Ours will be similarly judged.

The Great Work of our generation is the task of negotiating the rapids of human history, or what biologist E. O. Wilson calls a "bottleneck." It is a "crisis of crises," an interlocking set of problems, each part of which must be solved to resolve the whole. The problems of our time are now global, including poverty and hunger, environmental deterioration and rapid climate change, loss of species and economic prosperity, and security and justice. Taken together the global challenges of the twenty-first century have no historical precedent, although we ought to learn what we can from the experience of other transitional times. In short, we will have to remake our role in the natural world to recalibrate human intentions with the way the biophysical world works, a design problem. At a deeper level, the concern for our sustainability as a species represents a maturing of our kind to become "plain members and citizens" of an ecological community and trustees presiding midway between all that is past and all that is yet to come—a mystic chain of gratitude, obligation, charity, spirit, and hope.

The practical dimension of the Great Work ahead requires that we comprehend our problems as interlocking parts of a larger system and reverse a downward spiral of problems into an upward spiral of solutions. To do so, we must find leverage points in the system where relatively small changes have large positive results. This is not the same as finding a magic-bullet solution, but rather a creative rethinking of our situation. To illustrate, a rapid but coherent transition toward energy efficiency and renewable energy would:

Reduce dependence on Middle Eastern oil,
Lessen our military engagement in an unstable region,
Encourage a homegrown renewable energy industry,
Create millions of new jobs,
Reduce oil spills and water and air pollution,
Lower medical expenses and improve health,
Remove the influence of fossil energy companies on U.S. politics,
Contribute to stabilizing climate, thereby avoiding an avoidable catastrophe,
Improve our reputation and standing in the community of nations,
and so on . . .

Each of these collateral benefits of efficiency and renewable energy is well known and well documented. Nevertheless we are offered more nuclear power plants—which are potential targets for terrorists—more inefficient cars, more pollution, more coal mines, more oil wells, more risk, more oil wars, and ever greater environmental and economic costs.

Opinion polls show that the public is ready for the transition to a smarter energy policy, but nothing happens at the federal level. This and other examples that could be cited bring me back to the beginning. Before we get to the Great Work, we will have to put our house in order. The scope of our challenges will require collective, public choices that are first and foremost political. Something, indeed, has gone wrong in America and its causes lie in the way we are conducting the public business.

To candidly describe even a few of the present wrongs in U.S. politics, however, may sound shrill or even unpatriotic to some, especially during the "war on terrorism." But if not now, when? The vice president tells us that that this thing could go on for fifty years. I won't live that long, so I intend to speak my mind now. And democracy, as I understand it, begins with the right to say "wait just one cotton-pickin' minute!" and get a decent hearing. What I see is a disturbing pattern emerging that has less to do with combating terrorism than with using the fear of terrorism disguised as super-patriotism to promote a hard-right agenda and destroy progressive government and all opposition.

The president, once thought to be a public servant, asserts his right to wage preemptive wars against any nation he deems a threat. Neither Congress nor a fearful public rises to challenge. He orders an attack on Iraq even though the best evidence available showed that it posed no real threat to the United States. The *Washington Post,* the *New York Times,* CNN, NBC, ABC, CBS, MSNBC, and right-wing radio all serve as cheerleaders for his war. His national security advisor, Condoleezza Rice, apparently knew that Iraq in all likelihood did not have weapons of mass destruction prior to the invasion. (If so, withholding that evidence from the president is an impeachable offense and possibly treasonous.[2] If she did communicate that information to the president, he should be similarly charged for knowingly taking the country to war under false pretenses.) Dominated by the right wing, both houses of Congress remain agreeably supine. Rice is promoted to secretary of state with vigorous dissent from only a few Democrats. The evidence is reasonably clear that the president intended to invade Iraq long before the events of 9/11, but few in the press or television find that worthy of investigation.[3] No good answers are given for the failure of the White House to respond to multiple high-level warnings of an impending attack on the United States in 2001. The White House first tries to stop the investigation into the events of 9/11, then to restrict its scope, and then with the investigation underway, to withhold crucial evidence. The commission charged with investigating the events of 9/11, wishing to preserve harmony, refuses to assign blame for White House incompetence or worse.[4] The White House attorney argues in secret memorandums that the president is above the law, that the Geneva Convention is merely a quaint anachronism, and that torture is permissible for anyone suspected of terrorism. He is promoted to attorney general of the United States. The architects of the "shock and awe" war who demonstrated a lack of a foresight and a brazen incompetence that makes George Custer at Little Bighorn look really good are awarded the Medal of Freedom or are retained in office. No one is investigated, charged, or fired. Evidence that prisoners under military or CIA custody are often subjected to systematic humiliation, sexual degradation, physical abuse, and torture becomes irrefutable.[5] An unknown number have been tortured to death. A few in the lower ranks are tried, but the muddy footprints go far up the chain of command leading toward the Oval Office where no investigation is permitted. Republican senators like James Inhofe, a specimen from an earlier period of evolution, and right-wing bloviator Rush Limbaugh dismiss the issue as comparable to fraternity-boy pranks and attack those bringing the evidence of lawlessness. The vice president's company, Halliburton, is not required to go through the normal bidding procedures to win lucrative government contracts. Not even a whisper of dissent from those who otherwise advertise themselves as men of good judgment and fiscal probity.

At home the chasm between political spin and actual policy grows wider by the day. The so-called Clear Skies Initiative is a smokescreen for dirty air and yet another giveaway to the coal and oil industries. The words "healthy forests" veil yet another robbery from the public lands.[6] The administration of George W. Bush aims to dismantle the laws and regulations protecting the public health and environment, but by stealth and out of public sight.[7] The silence of the media, in particular, is deafening, for it too has been mostly bought or cowed.[8] Ethical standards in the U.S. Congress are rewritten to preclude serious investigation of systematic and widespread corruption by Tom Delay, the majority leader of the House. Evidence of voter fraud and manipulation of the vote in both the 2000 and 2004 elections continues to grow, but the mainstream media do not find that interesting.[9] The outing of a CIA agent, a federal crime, leads to the prosecution of reporters unconnected to the story but not to the arrest of any White House official or of Robert Novak, who did publish the story. A right-wing male escort mysteriously acquires a White House press pass and surfaces at presidential press conferences to ask puffball questions at opportune moments. No one is held to account, no one explains, and few in the media find either travesty worthy of investigation.

The list of malfeasances, mendacity, and incompetence go on and on. But there is, as they say, method in the madness. Beneath the words, evasions, and invasions there is a plan, of sorts, to use fear of terrorism and a state of permanent crisis (part fabrication, part real, and part a predictable reaction to U.S. policies to combat terrorism) to take care of the "base" of extremely wealthy, to mollify right-wing evangelicals, to increase the national debt thereby forcing Congress to dismantle social and domestic programs, and to extend the reach of empire. The goal is not a smaller government but a larger one redirected toward control and manipulation, a totally intimidated or wholly owned media, and a supine and vulnerable public. This is said to be "conservative," but Newt Gingrich identified it correctly when he called the right-wing agenda "revolutionary." It is a thoroughgoing reactionary coup aimed at remodeling the government to create an alliance between the military, intelligence agencies, corporations, a pliant media, and a one-party state.

Call it what you will, but something has gone dreadfully wrong in American politics. Many are becoming aware and are deeply concerned, but large numbers of Americans, otherwise well versed on the intimate lives of celebrities, seem befuddled at best and somnambulant at worst when it comes to politics. We are the most media-saturated but among the least informed people on Earth and this is no accident. We are ruled by a plutocracy, distracted by the entertainment industry, and are frequently misinformed by an increasingly concentrated news media that puts the pursuit of market share above telling the whole truth. Part symptom, part cause, we have state legislatures and a Congress with a lot of members who haven't read widely, thought deeply, or imagined much beyond their own pecuniary gain. The result is a leadership vacuum on the big issues of our time that is now filled with lobbyists for the rich and powerful who talk the language of populism while doing all in their power to undermine real democracy.

The Bush administration fights its war on terrorism in a way that will certainly increase enmity toward the United States and thereby increase the numbers of terrorists and deepen their sense of purpose. Diplomacy, nuance, subtlety, empathy for other cultures, and a knowledge of history are mocked. In his second inaugural address, George W. Bush announced a global crusade to spread freedom and democracy around the world, but democracy and the right to dissent and a free press at home are being systematically undermined. Its rhetoric notwithstanding, the present administration is proving to be the most reactionary, closed, and deceitful in our history, and that is saying a great deal.

Is this what Americans want? The evidence shows otherwise. Polls, for example, consistently show that most Americans want open government and the free flow of information, but the White House does not. Polls consistently show that Americans don't want dirty air or filthy water, but some well-connected industries do. Most Americans don't want poisons in their food, but agribusiness and chemical companies do. Most Americans would prefer not to run the considerable risks of climate change, but a few extremists do. Most Americans want health-care coverage for everyone, but the health-care industry does not. Most Americans don't want assault rifles on their streets, but the leadership of the National Rifle Association does. Most Americans don't want our nation to ignore old friends and allies and act as a global bully, but a few fantasize about empire in the "new American century." A sizeable majority of Americans would like to get to the heart of what ails us and remove money, once and for all, from the political process, but a few do not. None of us specifically voted for any of these things and few would support them given the truth and better alternatives, of which there are many. But for the time being, the few are in control.

The democratic processes that are supposed to connect the public will to government policy are broken and the reasons are not hard to find. There is, first, a marked decline in public accountability. In the Eisenhower years, for example, the revelation that a presidential advisor had received a vicuña coat was sufficient to force his resignation. By comparison George W. Bush famously asserts,

> I'm the commander—see, I don't need to explain—I do not need to explain why I say things. That's the interesting thing about being the president. Maybe somebody needs to explain to me why they say something, but I don't feel like I owe anybody an explanation.[10]

Louis XIV never said it better. Accountability, however, is a two-way street. Those entrusted with public office should intend to be accountable *and* they should be held accountable by an alert citizenry that demands authenticity, honesty, and transparency in the conduct of the public business.

Second, by a well-funded campaign of denigration we've been led to devalue the public and the political in favor of free markets, free trade, and a devil-take-the-hindmost kind of individualism. Economics of the worst kind has become a kind of secular religion for many on both the left and the right of the political spectrum. They believe that markets and free trade will fix virtually all of our public and political problems—if only we get government off our backs. Markets certainly can do some things, but if they do anything for children, grandchildren, communities, democracy, parks, environmental quality, climate stability, biological diversity, public health, literacy, fairness, justice, peace, democracy, or the long-term, it is purely accidental. Without regulation and direction markets will traffic in assault rifles or Bibles, poisons or vitamins, Humvees or hybrids, pornography or art—whatever the highest bidders want. And without a sense of irony, those much devoted to unfettered markets conveniently overlook that billions are spent for advertising and billions more to lobby for tax breaks and subsidies. The free market, much admired in theory, is not and never has been entirely free. At its extreme, the idea is a fraud. Markets, as Adam Smith knew, have always and everywhere required the restraints imposed by stable communities, rules, regulations, laws, and decent law-abiding people who honor contracts. The mania for free markets will someday be seen for what it is: a curious intellectual aberration but with destructive consequences for real people and real places.

Government, on the other hand, was created to advance larger aims and protect those things that should not be sold in any market, ever. If some things should not be sold, it follows that government, the guardian of those things, should not be up for sale either. But it is. Extremists, now in control of the White House, Congress, the courts, and much of the media, want to go further to repeal the hard-won social, environmental, and economic gains of the twentieth century and abort the idea that we, as citizens working through representative institutions, might do many things better in the twenty-first century. They intend to turn the clock back to a more brutal time and run government as if it were a business. Exactly which business they don't say. Is it Enron? Or WorldCom? Or Global Crossings? Or Arthur Anderson? Or maybe it's the vice president's own company, Halliburton, experts in overcharging us for their services and dodging public scrutiny.

Market fundamentalism and the denigration of the political, however, would not have been possible without a great deal of confusion about the meanings of words we use to describe our political life and public choices. George Orwell warned that the subversion of society begins with the corruption of its language. Words such as "conservative," "liberal," "patriotism," "taxation," "public," "government," and even "Christianity" have been twisted and distorted by those who stand to gain much from public perplexity. The angry fulminations and garish nonsense of the likes of Rush Limbaugh, Bill O'Reilly, Shawn Hannity, Ann Coulter, Michael Savage, and Grover Norquist serve as a smokescreen for a new generation of robber barons and the grand larceny now under way. Their carefully crafted veneer of angry populism is useful demagoguery that aims to heighten and then to exploit fears endemic to a rapidly changing society. While they distract the public, others rendered less visible are pillaging our children's future. American politics has seldom been nastier or nuttier and talk-show thuggery is assumed to be the only way to conduct public dialogue.

Looking to the horizon, the political, social, and economic topography grows steeper and more treacherous. We will soon see the mounting consequences of climate change, the loss of biological diversity, toxic pollution, the breakdown of entire ecosystems, rising population, growing poverty, terrorism, ecological refugees, political instability, and new diseases for which we have no good remedies. Rather than deal with these issues in a timely and systematic way as prudence and common sense would suggest, we've done a quarter-century equivalent of an Australian walkabout in which delay, denial, and dereliction have become the norm in our national politics. We now have to move as quickly as possible from fossil fuels to renewable energy and to establish sustainable practices in agriculture and forestry, rebuild habitable cities, construct an ecologically viable transportation system, protect biological diversity, create sustainable communities, safeguard air and water quality, eliminate toxics, and, not least, distribute wealth fairly within and between generations.[11] These, however, are not separate or separable things, but rather part of a larger pattern. They require us to understand the connections between how we provision ourselves with energy, food, and shelter and issues of economic prosperity, fairness, security, and democracy.

Are we up to the multiple challenges of building a fair and durable society and helping to lead the world in better directions than those now in prospect? Time will tell, but I believe that we are and that doing so fits with our best traditions. But it will require that we get our own house in order, and that means first and foremost the political task of rebuilding its democratic foundations and the atrophied habits of citizenship. The unfinished business of America is to extend and deepen our ideas of equality, positive freedom, decency, nonviolence, and commonwealth—a transformation that will one day temper individualism with the acknowledgment of our obligations and responsibilities; replace the extractive/consumer economy with a truly prosperous economy that protects the natural capital of soils, forests, and biotic diversity; and that will extend and broaden the idea of representation to include future generations and the larger web of life.

Like the American Revolution, this transformation will require people who understand that automatic obedience to power is merely subservience, that there can be no such thing as cheap patriotism. Democracy begins not when everyone is in agreement, but rather when one person stands up to disagree and is not shouted down. Real patriots know that we are bound together by the Constitution and the principles of justice, decency, and fairness. They know that patriotism is about building decent and prosperous communities and protecting the soils, forests, water, and wildlife as the rightful legacy of our children and theirs. And they know the ancient truths: that violence in all of its forms is wrong and ultimately self-defeating; that health, holy, healing, and wholeness are one and indivisible.

In Irish folklore the salmon is regarded as the wisest of creatures because it knows how to find its way home. That, in a way, is our challenge. Can we find our way back to a future in which our best traditions, highest values, and a sense of connection with place and posterity prevail? This book is dedicated to three pioneers of that future—practitioners of politics practiced as the art of visionary leadership. And because of them and thousands of others, some far-off day those looking back on our time may see this as our finest hour.

The chapters that follow are organized into three parts. The first section is about recent U.S. politics and the flourishing arts of denial. The picture it paints is neither pretty nor is it consistent with the highest ideals of our history. To the previous edition, I have added two essays written in light of the election of 2004. The first outlines the present crisis of democracy, here in this most evangelical of democracies, in light of the hopes and fears of James Madison. The second is an epistle of sorts to religious fundamentalists whose version of Christianity is, I think, a large part of what ails us because it has radically departed from what Christ actually taught. The second section of the book focuses on four aspects of the long-term issues contained in what has come to be called sustainability. To achieve sustainability, I believe, will require a more complicated and difficult transition than is often described and will stretch us in surprising and difficult ways to do what we will someday see as part of a more enlightened self-interest and that our descendents will someday regard as merely obvious choices. The third section is predicated on my belief that tinkering at the margins of our problems won't do. It is time to think more deeply about the intersection of global ecological realities with human frailties, possibilities, and obligations. The industrial, extractive economy and its politics cannot be sustained. But what alternatives do we have? I mention three. At the risk of being thought hopelessly nostalgic and backward looking, chapter eleven suggests that Wendell Berry's version of agrarianism remodeled to fit the postpetroleum world of the twenty-first century is worthy of serious consideration. A second suggestion is to amend the Constitution to protect the rights of future generations and thereby constrain our own, but in ways that are paradoxically beneficial. Chapters thirteen and fourteen argue that the future is in our hands.

No problem described herein is unsolvable; which is to say that we do not lack for technological remedies, better ideas, or even vision. But we do lack leadership commensurate with the challenges of our time. And that, finally, can be solved only by an alert, informed, and engaged citizenry that regards itself as a public.

Politics

one

James Madison's Nightmare

"Tis the times" plague, when madmen lead the blind.

—SHAKESPEARE, *King Lear*

James Madison was the most influential and prescient of that remarkable group of patriots that shaped the ideas underlying the American Revolution into a constitution and structure for the government of the United States. More than any of the Founding Fathers, he was the author of the U.S. Constitution and the Bill of Rights. In the *Federalist Papers,* number 10, Madison expressed his greatest fear: that all branches of government might one day be captured by a single faction "united and actuated by some common impulse of passion, or of interest, adverse to the rights of other citizens, or to the permanent and aggregate interests of the community" and thus would descend into tyranny. "The latent causes of faction are thus sown in the nature of man," but Madison aimed not to eliminate factionalism but to dilute its effects by enlarging the size of the republic and dividing power through a system of checks and balances, thereby reducing the chances that a single party could ever control the presidency, both houses of Congress, and the Supreme Court.

"Ambition," he wrote in *Federalist* number 51, "must be made to counteract ambition."

Madison was a short-term optimist, believing that it might be possible to maintain a representative democracy for a long time, given the division of power and the potential of the vast reaches of the North American continent to dilute regional interests. But he was also a realist who acknowledged human foibles and passions and the population growth that would one day render the New World much like the Old World.[1]

The election of 2004 set the United States on track to become a one-party state, with all branches of government controlled, not just by a single party, but by a highly disciplined, ideologically motivated faction within that party positioned at the extreme right-wing of American politics. After 215 years, Madison's nightmare has at last become a reality, but it's worse than he feared. That faction within a single party also controls the CIA, the military establishment, a majority of state houses, federal courts, and has bought or cowed much of the media, which the founders believed to be so essential to a viable democracy that they gave it special protection in the First Amendment. The controlling faction has thereby made itself—for a time—immune to the investigative power of an energetic free press, the outrage of a properly informed citizenry, and the prosecutorial reach of the law.

The story behind the rise of the extreme right in American politics has yet to be told. When it is, we will learn a great deal more about the people who gave the billions of dollars that funded right-wing think tanks, radio talk shows, and television "news" programs that resuscitated and spread the ideas of the robber barons, the social Darwinists, and the vision of Calvin Coolidge.[2] From the early 1970s on, they made common cause with the religious right, with the ancient haters of Franklin Roosevelt and the social programs of the New Deal, and with economic royalists to undermine the role of government as a countervailing power to corporations. They reviled the idea that government could improve the lives of ordinary people or protect the environment or establish a safety net for the victims of the corporate economy. They ran against "big government," but that was a lie. The record written in the federal budget and tax laws shows that big government is fine with them as long as it is used to reward corporations, police the citizenry, or further grow the military, but not when it works for the larger public interest.

The story seems to have begun with a 1971 memo from Richmond attorney and future Supreme Court justice Lewis Powell to the leadership of the U.S. Chamber of Commerce. Alarmed by the rise of the environmental, peace, and public-interest movements and the political turbulence of the late 1960s, Powell proposed that big business counterattack. The memo, titled "Attack on American Free Enterprise System," advised corporations to pursue a long-term strategy to reassert control. "Strength," as he put it, "lies in organization, in careful long-range planning and implementation, in consistency of action over an indefinite period of years, in the scale of financing available only through joint effort, and in the political power available through united action and national organizations."[3] Powell also proposed that the right should, in David Brock's words, "directly harass the media into conforming to its ideology."[4]

The Business Roundtable, created in 1972, became the command center to execute the strategy envisioned by Powell, but businessmen and conservative foundations created dozens of other organizations aimed at furthering their agenda, including the Heritage Foundation, the Pacific Legal Foundation, the Federalist Society, and the American Legislative Exchange Council. The single message they propagated through talk radio, seminars, television, glossy reports, and newspapers—that government is the problem and unfettered free enterprise the answer—was repeated like a mantra in every possible forum until it was duly etched on the American political mind. Executed with single-mindedness and plenty of cash, the counterattack succeeded beyond Powell's imagination, setting the stage for a systemwide coup that has shifted the center of U.S. politics far to the right, with only scattered and ineffective resistance from those who believe that government can be a progressive force to defend the public and its interests. The political exploitation of 9/11, the adroit manipulation of fear, and the purported "war on terror" did the rest.

Neither James Madison nor any of the other founders could have foreseen the rise of corporations and the threat they would one day pose to democracy. Such as they existed in the late eighteenth century, corporations were relatively small and subject to the control of states.

And neither Madison nor any of the other founders thought much about the environment for the simple reason that it did not pose any problem that they could see or foresee. The nearly one billion humans on the Earth equipped with the technology of the eighteenth century were small relative to the scale of the planet, and the science of ecology was still a century and a half distant. All of that has changed. Six billion four hundred million humans are now the dominant force driving global change. In the nearly fifteen minutes that it will take you to read this chapter one species will disappear, 375 acres will be made into desert, 4,500 tons of topsoil will be eroded, 18 acres of rainforest will be lost, 245,000 tons of carbon will enter the atmosphere, and four people somewhere on Earth will die from the effects of climate change. Hour by hour, day in, day out, week by week, year after year— the cumulative effect is a steady ratcheting down of the human prospect driven by the combined forces of ignorance, ideology, economics undisciplined by ecology, and greed-induced indifference. The environment is no longer just "out there," or another item on a long list of problems. It has become the linchpin issue connecting questions of security, economic prosperity, human health, and fairness. Environmental decisions about how we provision ourselves with food, energy, water, materials, and how we manage our waste will make us either more or less secure, prosperous, healthy, and just.

The fact is that those describing themselves as environmentalists have been mostly right about the big issues of our time. Rachel Carson, for example, was right about the ecological and health effects of the indiscriminate use of pesticides in the environment. Amory Lovins is right about the potential for energy efficiency and the fact that we have good alternatives to replace fossil fuels and every reason to do so. Wendell Berry has been right about the cultural, social, and environmental effects caused by the destruction of family farms and farm communities. Donella Meadows was right about the need to see our problems as components of larger systems. John Todd, Bill McDonough, Sim Van der Ryn, and Janine Benyus are right about the potential to design regenerative systems that mimic nature, thereby reducing environmental impacts and economic costs while improving our ability to withstand global disruptions. If the advice of these and dozens of others had become national policy, much as proposed in the *Global 2000* report of 1980, we would not have been nearly as reliant on distant supply lines, hence not nearly as vulnerable to terrorists as we were on 9/11.

Instead, a majority of American voters in 1980 bought the snake oil that it was "morning in America" and that we would not have to become ecologically smarter or more efficient in our use of resources. The reasons for our naiveté are complicated but in large part have to do with the fact that we are a lot less well informed than we ought to be. A 2002 Roper poll, for example, shows that only one-third of Americans can pass a basic test of environmental knowledge and that only 12 percent could pass an elementary test on the science and technology of energy. Of those voting for George W. Bush in the 2004 election, 75 percent believed that Saddam Hussein supported Al Qaeda in planning the 9/11 attacks; 73

percent believed that Saddam Hussein either had weapons of mass destruction or had a "major program" to create them.[5] How could so many be so trusting of power and so ignorant of the facts? The reasons are many, but one clue is found in a recent study by the National Endowment for the Arts showing that in the last decade reading across all income and education categories is down by 15 percent, while 80 percent are said to get their news from commercial television.[6]

Our confusions and lack of interest in politics and in the arts of democracy come at a particularly bad time in our history. We are nearing the end of the era of cheap oil and will have to make a rapid transition to a very different energy system. In 2002 the United States imported 53 percent of its oil and by the year 2020 that number is expected to rise to 72 percent. World oil extraction will soon peak and turn down, but the demand for oil will grow as China and other nations compete with us to fuel their burgeoning economies. That the largest remaining reserves of oil are in the Middle East creates the likelihood for potentially deadly geopolitical struggles in a politically unstable region far into the future.[7] We have locked ourselves into an unnecessary, wasteful, and dangerous cycle of inefficiency, dependency, high costs, and conflict. The efficiency of our cars in 2002 was no better than it was in 1980 partly because the average weight of new vehicles is two tons. Yet we seem unable to make the obvious connection between the efficiency of what we drive, the end of the era of cheap fossil fuels, terrorism, the wars we ask our sons and daughters to fight, and the environmental and political conditions that we will leave behind for our grandchildren.

On the horizon are the clear warning signs of climate change caused by our combustion of fossil fuels. Arctic ice and the ice sheet covering Greenland are in full retreat. The number of climate-driven weather extremes is rising sharply: more storms, more violent storms, record droughts and heat waves, rising seas, melting permafrost, migrating species, and the spread of tropical diseases into areas where they were previously unknown.[8] All of these are consistent with the possibility that we are driving climate into a new and, perhaps, dangerous phase. The Intergovernmental Panel on Climate Change projects temperature increases in this century that will range between a low of 2.5 and a high of 10.4 degrees Fahrenheit, but more recent findings suggest that that estimate could be far too low. A growing body of evidence indicates that sooner than later things will come undone, but those in authority blindly continue to believe that we can turn the thermostat of the Earth up several notches and nothing else will happen. But that is not the world that we see on the evening news or of which we read in the morning papers, where small changes often trigger large results.

The founders devised a government that divided power, checked ambition, and thwarted tyranny. But it aimed, as well, to solve the practical problems facing the young country. We have entered the third century of that experiment in radically altered circumstances. However large the problems faced by the founders, our problems are now global, with consequences that stretch to the far horizon, yet our political capacity to solve problems is being dismantled. For those who wish for a habitable and decent planet, what do we do?

One strategy is to do nothing different, expecting a miracle rather like the scientist in a well-known Sidney Harris cartoon who stands with a colleague before a long equation on the blackboard, the halves of which are connected by the words, "then a miracle occurs." His advice to his colleague to be "more explicit in step two" is good for us as well. We need to be explicit about our political intentions and how these are to come about.

A second strategy is to try to reach out to those on the other side of the issues in order to start a reasonable dialogue in a spirit of good will. Rather like the denial of every battered woman convinced that the last beating was somehow her fault, "reasonable" progressives wish to convert right-wing extremists by using yet more logic, more data, the power of kindness and reasonableness and by moving ever farther to the right. The strategy is captured in a Gary Larson *Far Side* cartoon that shows a huge alligator crashing onto the rear of a rowboat and about to devour Ernie while a woman in the upraised prow shouts to "rub his belly!" But there is a notable difference whether Ernie rubs the belly of the beast from the inside or the outside. So it is with progressives presently being served up for lunch by the right-wing being advised to accommodate, be reasonable, and go along.

We need a better strategy than one founded on hoping or placating—a third approach that joins politics, science, and values with the kind of courage and toughness that we associate with Abraham Lincoln or Winston Churchill. The starting point is to improve our political effectiveness, restore the vitality of democratic institutions, and reassert public control over common public property in the airwaves. From poll data over three decades we know that a large majority of Americans consistently support environmental causes but often fail to connect those values with their market choices and their votes. The fact is that the political mechanisms that connect public preferences with public policy and those bridging our roles as citizens and consumers are broken and must be repaired. There is hard political work to do and much of it must be directed toward restoring a functioning democracy and a well-informed citizenry. I have no blueprint to offer, but I do offer some components of a strategy, beginning with how we position environmental causes in the public arena. The talking heads of television or the headless voices of talk radio tell us that we are divided between red and blue, conservative and liberal. I don't believe it and you shouldn't either. All thinking and reasonably informed Americans are a bit of both: conservative on some issues and liberal on others. At our best we are a pragmatic people who aim to solve problems, not ideologues of left or right. Typically we want neither government intrusion in our lives, nor irresponsible corporations. We don't want government in our bedrooms, a libertarian value; but we do want the mail delivered, our children to be well educated, and the roads maintained, and those require government. But there is much to be gained by confusing people and hyping their fears and resentments in order to divide and conquer. All of us—liberals, conservatives, and independents alike—breathe the same air, drink the same water, and depend on the same ecological systems. A more thoughtful view of our politics would bisect the right/left line with one running at a right angle from the present to the future. In that perspective, the interests of our grandchildren and theirs becomes paramount. Liberals and conservatives alike can agree that we ought to clean up our own ecological messes, not leave them for our children and theirs. That belief runs back to the origins of conservatism in Edmund Burke and those of liberalism in the writings of Thomas Jefferson, both of whom argued that it was wrong for one generation to encumber subsequent generations with its waste, profligacy, and debt. That logic ought to apply to all forms of encumbrance, including ecological debts of a degraded biosphere and unstable climate.

Second, for all of the reasons that George Orwell portrayed in his book *1984*, it's time to take our public language back from the right-wing media. The word "liberal," which has been purposely corrupted, for example, is a noble word with an illustrious history. It means breadth of view, not narrow-mindedness, and the protection of personal liberty whether threatened by governments *or* by corporations. Liberals gave us child-labor laws, public education, the eight-hour work day, social security, civil rights laws, freedom of information, equal rights for women, the minimum wage, environmental protection, Medicare and Medicaid, and a successful war against Fascism. It was liberals who contained Communism. Conservatives of the time opposed all of these policies and efforts. Similarly, the word "patriot" once designated those willing to show physical *and* moral courage in the defense of the country, but has recently come to mean a great deal less, as if there were such a thing as cheap, bumper-sticker patriotism. The word "taxation" has also become a term of abuse. But fairly assessed—put to good uses that are otherwise not achievable in the market—taxes are, as Oliver Wendell Holmes once put it, the price we pay for civilization, not an unwarranted taking of private wealth. The manipulation of words and symbols by extremists has become an art form designed to confuse, baffle, and exploit public gullibility in order to further enrich the already wealthy. How will our grandchildren, who will bear the brunt of climate destabilization, regard pollster Frank Luntz's advice to Republicans that "the scientific debate is closing, but not yet closed. There is still a window of opportunity to challenge the science"?[9] By what words will our descendents describe such dereliction?

Third, a political strategy would aim to restore the "high wall" the founders placed between religion and the state written in the First Amendment.[10] They knew what the extreme right in American politics has forgotten, which is that the combination of religion and politics is a prescription for disaster.[11] The founders were mostly Deists (not religious as, say, Pat Robertson would define the word) with a keen sense of history and a deep understanding of human nature. They remembered Cromwell and understood how easily public affairs could be corrupted by those believing themselves to be possessors of absolute truth. But their good sense built into the First Amendment is being undermined by radical-right evangelicals who intend to create their own version of the Taliban. House majority leader Tom DeLay, for one, intends to convert America into a "God-centered nation" that would actively promote right-wing Christianity and what he deems to be Christian values. Others are even less subtle. Evangelist George Grant says frankly that "Christian politics has as its primary intent the conquest of the land—of men, families, institutions, bureaucracies, courts, and governments for the

Kingdom of Christ."[12] He and other evangelicals propose to undo the separation of church and state. This could be dismissed as inconsequential except that the religious right has achieved a remarkable hold on American politics. According to Glenn Scherer, "forty-five senators and 186 representatives in 2003 earned 80 to 100 percent approval ratings from the nation's three most influential Christian right advocacy groups." Equally worrisome, many fundamentalist Christians believe that the end times are upon us, and accordingly are not inclined to worry about pollution, deforestation, or climate change, which they interpret as signs of Christ's imminent return. But they are oblivious to the reality that they are bringing about an "end times" that has nothing to do with biblical prophecy.

Fourth, the First Amendment also says that "Congress shall make no law . . . abridging the freedom of speech, or of the press." The founders gave special attention to the press, believing that a well-informed public that exercised its right to speak and participate in politics was the foundation for democracy. "A popular government without information or the means to acquire it," as Madison put it, "is either prologue to a farce or a tragedy or perhaps both." We live in a more complicated information environment than the founders could have anticipated, making the principle of a free press even more important. In this light it is no small matter that control of the airwaves, part of the public commons, is dominated by fewer and fewer corporations. The "fairness doctrine," which once required radio and TV stations to air all sides of controversial issues, was overturned by President Reagan's Federal Communications Commission in 1987, a decision based on an earlier decision by the U.S. Court of Appeals for the District of Columbia in a 2-1 decision (the two being right-wing judges Robert Bork and Antonin Scalia). As a result, media companies are no longer required to present all sides of public issues as a condition for their license and can use the public airwaves to present unfair, inaccurate, and one-sided views of issues and call it "fair and balanced." The Telecommunications Act of 1996 compounded the problem by allowing vertical integration of radio and television stations and newspapers in the same media markets. This has meant that the news Americans hear is increasingly homogenized, stripped of political content, and delivered by only six major news outlets that compete for market share by entertaining audiences, not by using investigative reporting and in-depth coverage of complicated and contentious issues. By comparison, in 1980 there were fifty major outlets.[13] The news has become just another commercial commodity delivered by media conglomerates competing for the largest possible share of public attention. It's not surprising, then, that news increasingly resembles entertainment or that sensationalism and outright propaganda have replaced serious reporting.

Other problems follow. Because their districts are made safe by gerrymandering, few members of Congress ever lose an election and so have little incentive to moderate extreme positions on controversial issues.[14] The result is a level of acrimony that is almost without precedent in our history. The financing of political campaigns by corporations and wealthy donors is an ongoing scandal, corrupting democracy and public policy alike. The United States has become a garrison state, spending more on weapons and war than the next twenty-one nations combined, taking money from education, the environment, renewable energy, medical care, urban renewal, public transportation—the foundation for genuine security and a secure prosperity. Corporations, not mentioned in the Constitution, have assumed a power that would have appalled the founders. Even as early as 1864 Abraham Lincoln expressed fears for what lay ahead:

> As a result of the war, corporations have been enthroned and an era of corruption in high places will follow, and the money power of the country will endeavor to prolong its

reign by working upon the prejudices of the people until all wealth is aggregated in a few hands and the Republic is destroyed.)

Lincoln's fears have come to pass. Corporations, an abstraction, are now protected under the Bill of Rights as if they were private citizens—which explains the origins of a great deal of economic and political mischief. The distribution of income has once again become as skewed toward the wealthiest as it was prior to the stock market crash of 1929. The largest transfer of wealth from the poor and middle classes to the rich in history took place between 1980 and 2005. None of this can be blamed on Republicans alone. The Democrats have done their part by being an ineffective opposition party and an uncertain trumpet for the causes of the poor, fairness, the environment, peace, and the interests of their own children. Without a coherent and compelling alternative vision and the grit to act on it, they risk extinction as a political party.

Madison feared that the Constitution might last only for a time before it all came undone and the forces of tyranny became dominant once again. He was a realist about human nature and the human tendency to divide into factions. But he also believed that the architecture of government and particularly the division of power in a system of checks and balances would delay the inevitable. The question is whether we have the will and ingenuity in this late hour to prove that his fears were unfounded. The answer hangs in the balance. The philosophy of democracy is laid out in the defining documents of the Republic: the Declaration of Independence, the Constitution, the *Federalist Papers,* the Bill of Rights, and the Four Freedoms of Franklin Roosevelt.[15] They shaped us as a people and placed at the heart of this experiment in self-government the ideas that the people should have a say in the conduct of the public business, that all of us are equal before the law, that those who exercise power are to be held accountable and can be discharged by the people voting in free and unfettered elections, that information ought to be transparent and freely available to all, and that government should be neutral toward any and all religions.

We are being reshaped by other documents in ways that Madison feared. A 5-4 Supreme Court decision (*Bush v. Gore*, 2000) stopped the counting of legitimate votes cast in an election in Florida tainted by fraud. But that decision was limited by the Court to apply only to that one case, making a mockery of the law. The same Court supported the vice president's refusal to say who was at the table when the National Energy Plan was drafted, undermining our right as citizens to know how our business is conducted and by whom. The Patriot Act of 2001 effectively strips citizens accused of terrorism of their protections under the Bill of Rights. Not least, the president's national security strategy claims the right to preemptively attack any country that he alone deems a threat, thereby voiding the constitutional provision that only Congress can declare war. Whatever the reality of terrorism, the fear of it is now used to subvert democratic processes and public accountability and to concentrate power in the hands of the most secretive, authoritarian, ideological, and extremist administration in American history.

Through civil war, world wars, and depression, democracy in America has lasted 215 years, far longer than Madison thought it might. On November 2, 2004, that great experiment became something else more sinister, unmoored from the Constitution and divorced from our highest values. After seven generations, democracy as conceived by the Founding Fathers was finally undone by a combination of imperial ambition; the lack of an effective opposition party; an ineffective and corrupted press; corporate greed; political shortsightedness; a spirit of meanness; and a fearful, media-saturated but poorly informed public. We the people have allowed ourselves to be deceived and made subjects in an empire that operates beyond the constraints of law, morality, democracy, and a decent regard for the opinions of other nations. The hallmarks of empire are there for all to see: secrecy, manipulation of the facts, outright lies, financial dereliction, the lack of accountability by the highest officials, assassinations, and prisons hidden from public view where the arts of torture are practiced. Perhaps political theorist Sheldon Wolin was right when he concluded that "capitalism [produced] human beings unfitted for democratic citizenship."[16] But I am not yet prepared to make that final concession to the makers and benefactors of empire. I do not believe that this, or any, country can be run for long on mendacity, blood, and debt or that our good sense has been eroded beyond recovery. We are a better people than that.

For those wishing to restore democracy at home while we are supposedly fighting for it elsewhere, the long-term objectives are clear: eliminate money from politics; reassert public control of the airwaves; restore a free, locally owned press; repair the wall the founders placed between church and state; educate the people once again to be discerning citizens; and use our buying power as consumers to declare our independence from fossil fuels and begin the transition toward energy efficiency and solar energy. How can we do such things? The same way all great and noble things have been accomplished— with patience, courage, conviction, relentless ingenuity, and a mastery of the art of strategy. The soft underbelly of the Bush-Cheney-Rove-Limbaugh empire includes all thoughtful conservatives disturbed by fiscal recklessness and imperial pretensions; all honest persons offended by mendacity, bombast, and conniving that diverts us from our real problems; all true Christians sufficiently alert to notice the discrepancy between the words and life of the Prince of Peace and our foreign and domestic policies. And we have no time to lose and no energy to spend on despair.

two

Authentic Christianity and the Problem of Earthly Power

I was raised in a Christian family. My father was a conservative Presbyterian minister and president of a church-related college. His father was an evangelist who traveled the country holding revival meetings, during one of which he gave the christening prayer for Rachel Carson's baptism.[1] He eventually returned to his hometown, built a church, and remained until his death as the much-revered pastor of the Tabernacle Associate Reformed Presbyterian Church in downtown Charlotte. On my mother's side, my great-grandfather was a missionary in Mexico. Two of his grandsons, my uncles, were Presbyterian preachers and I still regard them as among the most saintly people I've ever known.

As a child I was taught that with Christ the veil parted for a moment in time to allow humankind a glimpse of eternity and to hear the voice of God. The heart of the Christian faith that I learned is found in the Sermon on the Mount and in the doctrine of divine forgiveness, because all, without exception, have fallen short of the glory of God. It is a faith of humility, not one of power and domination. The writer of Corinthians 1:13 places charity above even faith and hope. Christians are asked to love the Lord God with all of their soul, hearts, and minds, which is to say that faith must be both heartfelt and thought through. It is a faith that beckons its followers away from materialism. Alert to Christ's rejection of the temptation to seek political power, Christians ought to engage in politics cautiously, if at all. It is an inclusive faith; Christ's invitation is to all who hunger and thirst for righteousness without qualification whatsoever. It is a faith that balances the deficit of personal merit with divine grace and, in that largesse, requires our forgiveness of those who trespass against us. Christianity forbids judging the speck in another's eye lest we miss the beam in our own.

The Bible that I read, however, is complicated, paradoxical, and sometimes contradictory. There is no way to reconcile it all into some superdivine whole that makes any sense at all without making a mockery of one's God-given intelligence. How are we to reconcile the cruelties and indulgences of the Old Testament, for example, with Jesus' admonition to love our neighbors? Even the sayings of Jesus, some apparently added many years after his crucifixion, are sometimes contradictory. Honest Christians can accordingly disagree about many things, but not about Jesus' call to love others as we love ourselves, to do good to our enemies, to turn the other cheek, to reject violence in all of its forms, and to care for the poor. This is a hard faith and it runs against the human grain, nowhere as clearly as in the realm of political power. And this is the problem of contemporary Christianity.

In recent decades an angrier, meaner, and more dubious strain of Christianity has emerged on the far right of American life and politics.[2] Adherents describe it as fundamentalism or traditionalism, but its roots only go back to novel doctrines of "dispensational premillennialism" cooked up in the nineteenth century by one John Nelson Darby and later propagated through C. I. Scofield's Reference Bible that sold tens of thousands of copies, mostly in the South. Few Americans have ever heard of either man, but they have heard of their later disciples who include Pat Robertson and Jerry Falwell.[3] Theirs is a religion long on prophecies of the end times, said to be hidden in the book of Revelation, and short on love, forgiveness, tolerance, and charity. Like all fundamentalists, those of the right-wing persuasion offer the dubious proposition that heads they win, tails you lose. Adherents of the more extreme Tim LaHaye "left behind" variety display a remarkable eagerness to watch billions of unbelievers (anyone who disagrees) writhe in agony in the burning lake of fire where their vengeful God has casually tossed them. And roasting your enemies does have some historical precedent among the true believers of earlier times.

This new strain of Christianity is narrowly legalistic, judgmental, antiscience, authoritarian, patriarchal, supernationalistic, militaristic, and not closely affiliated with the actual gospel of Jesus Christ. But it is now a substantial part of the Republican Party's base—the heart of what some describe as "red America." If right-wing evangelicals did not necessarily swing the 2004 election to George W. Bush, there is no doubt about their fervor and political power.[4] In my home state of Ohio, for example, evangelicals for Bush turned out in high numbers, motivated predominantly by opposition to gay marriage and abortion while ignoring authentic issues like unemployment, economic justice, a questionable war, the destruction of the environment, and a political process corrupted by money.

Not all evangelicals, by any means, are conservative. Many are progressive and have spoken eloquently in opposition to war, poverty, tax breaks for the wealthy, and environmental destruction.[5] But they are nowhere as visible, organized, well funded, or influential in the corridors of power as those who say that they intend to make Christianity—their version of it—the religion of the land, a litmus test for holding public office, and the benchmark for public policy. But all who intend to follow the author of the Sermon on the Mount are obliged to heal the wounds in this country, promote peace, work for justice, and preserve Creation.

This essay is written as an appeal specifically to those who describe themselves as right-wing evangelicals, but it applies no less to mainstream Christians. I write candidly but hope, nonetheless, that what I say will be heard in a constructive spirit. I have no illusion, however, that healing antagonisms carefully nurtured for decades into a "cultural war" will be easy to do or will happen soon, but we can hope for a future of deeper understanding, mutual respect, and charity for all. I will begin with a disturbing illustration of the problem.

On October 29, immediately before the presidential election of 2004, the British medical journal *Lancet* published a study from the School of Public Health at Johns Hopkins University reporting that U.S. military actions in Iraq had killed more than one hundred thousand noncombatant Iraqi civilians—mothers, young children, elderly men and women ripped apart by U.S. bombs and bullets often made from depleted uranium that will bring still more death for years to come. One of the authors of the report said, "we're quite sure that the estimate of 100,000 is a conservative estimate."[6] The report appeared in the back pages of the *New York Times* and made hardly a ripple in the news of the day. If mentioned by either the Bush or Kerry campaigns, I didn't hear it. I doubt that it was discussed on right-wing talk radio except to accuse its authors of lacking "patriotism." If the report troubled conservative evangelicals, in particular, they remained silent.

If the report is, say, half wrong and we've killed "only" fifty thousand innocent men, women, and children, the fact remains that we have slaughtered tens of thousands with hardly so much as a twitch of national remorse—and there is no end to the killing in sight. Here at home, we continue to talk about "family values" while destroying families elsewhere in a war that many Christians supported in the belief that they were being told the truth by honest and competent leaders. It is time to ask with as much candor as possible, what kind of people have we become?

One answer is that we are a violent and vengeful people. Having lost more than three thousand of our own on 9/11, we felt justified to exact revenge, even on those not implicated. In the aftermath of the attack, we declared war on terrorists, but we had a choice to pursue the perpetrators as international criminals without a declaration of war. That course, however, would have required international cooperation and would have done relatively little to inflate U.S. military spending, now more than $447 billion per year or $14,000 per second. The pronouncement of war empowered the Bush administration to do things—at home and abroad—that we the people have not yet grasped, including the systematic and widespread use of torture. Some Americans were mesmerized for a time by a kind of cowboy movie lingo emanating from high places—"dead or alive," "bring 'em on," "axis of evil," "shock and awe," "we'll do whatever it takes," "mission accomplished."

Again, anyone wishing to understand what is happening would do well to read or reread George Orwell's *1984*. In Orwellian fashion the emergency was used as a pretext to whip up a national mood of revenge and to establish the right of the president to launch preemptive wars whenever he deemed it necessary. The safeguards of international law and constitutional rights for anyone said to be an enemy combatant were suspended, leading to egregious violations of human rights at Abu Ghraib and other military detention facilities. The Bill of Rights, fifty years of bipartisan foreign policy consensus, and the standards of international law were tossed aside while anyone brave enough to ask obvious and inconvenient questions was dismissed as unpatriotic. Administration officials talk about a fifty-year war against "terrorists" in a way that Orwell would have immediately understood. Nothing is quite as useful for those in power wishing to escape being held accountable as dependably loathsome enemies. Terrorists, or their shadows, can be used to distract a fearful public and to undermine rational thought that is essential to democracy while dissenters are reviled. It is a very old and very sad story.

Another answer is that we have become a nation of dolts mostly preoccupied with spending, sports, speed, entertainment, and the lives of celebrities and are no longer able to think attentively about political issues or to comprehend the effects of our actions in the world. A large percentage of Americans seem incapable of separating fictitious words from the reality of actual policies. After 9/11 few understood the causes of the attack on the United States or remembered our historic involvement with both Osama bin Laden and Saddam Hussein. The fact is that we had armed, financed, and trained both men when they were our allies in other, long-forgotten conflicts. The United States helped to make them what they later became. And from time to time chickens do come home to roost, a process that national security analysts call "blowback."

We aren't just forgetful. Perhaps only a third of Americans make the obvious connections between the gross energy inefficiency of our cars, the reasons behind our involvement in the swamp of Middle Eastern politics, and the catastrophic realities of climate change looming ahead. The fact is clear for all who wish to see that as a nation we are up to our neck in alligators in the Middle East because we lack the wit to eliminate our need for imported oil by developing superior and easily available technologies as part of a more resilient and more prosperous economy. The reasons are not hard to find: selling fossil fuels is a $2 trillion a year global business and we have a president and vice president whose personal fortunes, outlooks, and politics have been shaped by oil and by the particular greed and blindness that it engenders. Maybe our national IQ has been impaired by watching too much television concentrated in the hands of six major news outlets and increasingly dominated by strident right-wing commentators who never fail to complain about the insidious power of an all but vanished "liberal media."[7]

A third possibility, favored by those calling themselves neoconservatives, is that empire is our destiny and therefore a matter of right and idealists had better get used to it. As imperialists, we no longer need to show a decent regard for the opinions of other nations and humankind generally, as Thomas Jefferson once proposed. After all, we are a global colossus with more than seven hundred military bases around the world. But we ought to see that acquiring and managing an empire is a risky, expensive, and eventually futile business.[8] It's a fool's errand that will bring death, sorrow, and ruin in its wake. With today's technology and access to a good hardware store, any two-bit bunch of terrorists, malcontents, or just clever serial killers can cause havoc to our vulnerable and overextended lines supplying us with energy, food, water, and materials. We, the people of the United States of America, are vulnerable in more ways than we can count and no amount of military spending can erase that fact. Why then do we continue to provoke and insult other nations and peoples making ourselves an even larger target for terrorism? But we do, and as a result have quickly made ourselves the most feared and hated nation on Earth. Polls consistently show that our reputation in the world is at the lowest point in our history and is still falling.

A truly Christian people would not be vengeful, foolish, or ambitious for empire. Christians cannot indulge themselves in revenge; that is a right reserved for higher hands. Christians have an obligation to be informed and to think things through—to be as innocent as doves but as wise as serpents. That requires being informed enough to see through spin, evasions, lies, and half-truths. Christians should be wise enough to understand how the conduct of our nation's business fits with Christ's teachings of mercy, justice, and forgiveness. And true Christians cannot support empire, particularly one aimed to preserve U.S. control of foreign oil.

Beyond America's quest for empire lies an unsettling reality. Americans are 4 percent of the world's population, but use 25 percent of the planet's resources. We are also among the least energy efficient of the developed nations. As a result we are responsible for a quarter of the greenhouse gases that are changing climate catastrophically and with consequences that each year become more visible and painful. The World Health Organization, for example, estimates that 150,000 people die each year because of extreme weather events driven by climate change.[9] We are also the most wasteful people on Earth, leaving behind a legacy of poison and ecological ruin. After a century of promiscuous chemistry, our children bear a bodily burden of 190 toxic chemicals with health effects that are mostly unknown. Childhood diseases including asthma and autism are epidemic and we don't know why. We are the wealthiest nation on Earth, but rank among the lowest of industrialized nations on measures of wealth distribution, longevity, health care, and literacy. We, the richest people on Earth, spend more on pet food and cosmetic surgery ($26.6 billion) than we do on foreign aid ($15.8 billion). Once the world's leader in environmental protection, we have accepted a political regime that is systematically subverting environmental laws and protections, turning the clock back to a more benighted era.[10] We have more people in the criminal justice system (6.9 million) than any other nation.[11] We watch more television but seem to know less than people in Europe and Japan. And we are now the fattest people on Earth. To be sure, this is not all that we are, but America has become a paradox of noble ideals, promise, raw power, violence, extremes of wealth and poverty, gullibility, mendacity, and confusion.

On issues of environment, economic justice, health care, and peace, where are conservative evangelicals or even mainstream Christians for that matter? The hard truth is that they are seldom to be found. Instead, many have chosen to focus on issues that to our great-grandchildren will appear as odd or deranged. Opposition to abortion and gay marriage, glib talk about the imminence of the end times, and the need to seize political power are the issues of the day and all have become a form of idolatry. Let me be more specific.

1. Framed as "the right to life" on one hand and "a woman's right to choose" on the other, the issue of abortion cannot be resolved. For the sake of discussion, I am willing to dismiss the complexities of deciding the exact point at which a fetus can be said to possess a soul. For the moment, I am further willing to suspend the argument that women have a right to make their own reproductive decisions. But in return I ask defenders of the right to life only to be consistent lest principle be merely a thing of convenience selectively applied, which is to say no principle at all. If the right to life is absolute, does that not mean that children now alive should be protected with a fervor at least equal to that bestowed on the unborn by ensuring that they are well loved and have the basics of health care, nutrition, schooling, and decent housing? If the right to life is absolute, does that not rule out the death penalty? If the right to life is sacrosanct, how can Christians support the sale of assault weapons, which are good for nothing but killing people? If the right to life is paramount, doesn't that mean that we ought to seek nonviolent ways to resolve international conflicts? And if the right to life is important, should it not also apply to the preservation of other life forms presently disappearing by the thousands each year? These are not tangential issues but the heart and soul of a consistent and principled defense of life.

2. In the election of 2004 much was made of gay marriage. For those wishing to reelect the president, it served as a "wedge issue" aimed at "energizing the base." Conservative evangelicals by and large oppose gay marriage, supporting the exclusive sanctity of marriage between men and women. The scriptures, however, do not say a great deal about issues of sexual orientation and say nothing at all about gay marriage. More to the point, Christ said nothing on the subject

and cannot be quoted to particularly good effect either way. For evangelicals, the issue is more complicated because the sanctity of marriage is undermined by divorce rates that appear to run as high among conservative evangelicals as in the wider public.[12] The fact is that the sanctity of marriage is undermined by many things, including corporate advertising that routinely uses sexual imagery in television, movies, magazines, on the Internet, and in advertising to sell us more stuff. But conservative evangelicals speak hardly a word of protest about the excesses of corporate power and corruption. And it's ironic that people said to be much devoted to getting government off our backs would wish to put it into our bedrooms.

3. Evangelical conservatives make much about a battle of Armageddon and the impending end times. It has become a kind of fetish or obsession. The truth is that no one can know what is God's alone to know: whether, when, and how prophecy will be fulfilled. Those who assert otherwise pretend to know what they cannot know, aiming, often, to exploit the gullible. Whatever the motivation, the effect has been to make evangelicals careless stewards of our forests, soils, wildlife, air, water, seas, and climate, which is to say God's Creation and their children's rightful inheritance. That indifferent stewardship is bringing on an end time of ecological ruin that has no basis in biblical prophecy and can be no part of God's plan. It is, rather, the result of a profound indifference to life, which is to say a sin against Creation and a crime against humanity. Further, careless talk about the imminence of Armageddon suggests a darker fascination with death, militarization, and violence that is alien to all that Christ taught. We have it on high authority that between life and death, we are called to choose life, that we and our children might live abundantly.

4. Conservative evangelicals have become an active political force on the right-wing of U.S. politics. In doing so, they have made an unholy alliance with the powers of this world.

But nothing in Christ's teaching justifies such an alliance. Tempted, Jesus refused to assume political power, but the church has not always followed his example. Two thousand years of history show that the union of religious zealotry and the secular power of the state brings with it inquisitions, wars, intrigue, death, and ruin. In our own history the founders, intending to create a tolerant and peaceful society, set an absolute barrier between church and state in the First Amendment to the Constitution. They were mostly Deists, skeptical of doctrine, not Christians in the militant and self-assured way of, say, Pat Robertson or Jerry Falwell. But many evangelicals speak longingly of a time when a unified conservative evangelical church will have dominion over the government of the United States and the Constitution, creating its own version of the Taliban-ruled state.

Against the example of Christ, the warnings of history, and the wisdom of the Constitution, conservative evangelicals have entered into an alliance with the vendors of fossil fuels, the climate changers, the polluters, the sellers of weapons, the military, the imperialists, the exploiters, the political dirty tricksters, the spin artists, those willing to corrupt scientific truth for political gain, and those for whom law and the Constitution are merely scraps of paper. These are their confederates, making conservative evangelicals accomplices of the forces sweeping us toward more and more terrible violence, the avoidable catastrophes of climate change and ecological ruin, a police state, and injustice. To be certain, the powers will say whatever conservative evangelicals wish to hear about abortion, prayer in school, gay marriage, flag burning, and will even appoint judges of their liking. They will attend prayer breakfasts and give stirring speeches professing their love for Jesus. But they play conservative evangelicals for fools and use them with utter contempt to conceal the grand larceny under way. They will continue to loot the country and its people by shifting taxes onto the middle classes and poor, moving jobs overseas, undercutting the laws that protect environment and human health, waging wars in distant places using the sons and daughters of the poor as cannon fodder, and destroying our democracy, talking all the while about family values and morality. They ask only that their supporters be blind, gullible, ill informed, and unable to relate Christ's life and teachings to their actions, which is to say, be a people ripe for the plucking.

Christianity is a hard and paradoxical religion. We have it on high authority that the race is never to the swift, nor the battle to the strong. At their best, Christians comfort the afflicted and afflict the comfortable. Americans are now a comfortable people in a growing sea of violence, ecological ruin, poverty, and oppression. As a people of wealth, power, and might, we have become a very different nation than we once may have been. Thirty years ago, toward the end of another war, a brilliant theologian and lawyer, William Stringfellow, wrote words that speak even more poignantly to us today:

> A quarter of a century after the ostensible defeat of Nazi totalitarianism, the morality of Nazism thrives in American circumstances which were, at war's end, already hospitable to death and the idolatry of death in the nation.[13]

He went on to describe the president of that day, Richard Nixon, "as a victim and captive of the principalities and powers."

We have great difficulty seeing ourselves as others do and as others will someday. What they see and what others will see when the full record of our time is known is not and will not be flattering to our national image as a benign, generous, brave, noble, and Christian people. No nation as violent, as ecologically destructive, as hard-hearted, as self-satisfied, and as greedy as we have become can truly claim to be a Christian nation. We have made ourselves into a nation of violence, destruction, greed, and pride—far from the words and life of Christ. But there is hope at the heart of the Christian faith through humility, confession, forgiveness, and redemption. We are called as persons and as a nation only to be just, merciful, and to walk humbly with our God. Christianity, authentic Christianity, is a hard standard.

three

Walking North on a Southbound Train

A great storyteller I know once told about a fox that appears at the edge of a clearing in which a dog is tethered to a pole. The fox begins to run in circles just outside the radius of the dog's tether, followed by the frantically barking dog. After a few laps the fox has managed to tie the dog to the tether at which point he struts in to devour the dog's food while the helpless mutt looks on. Something like that has happened to all of us who believe nature and ecosystems to be worth preserving and that this is a matter of obligation, spirit, true economy, and common sense. Someone or something has run us in circles, tied us up, and is eating our lunch.[1] It is time to ask who and why and how we might respond. Here is what we know:

1. Despite occasional success, overall we are losing the epic struggle to preserve the habitability of the Earth. The overwhelming fact is that virtually all important ecological indicators show decline. The human population increased threefold in the twentieth century and will likely grow further before leveling off at 8 to 11

billion. The loss of species continues and will likely increase in coming decades. Human-driven climatic change is now underway and is occurring more rapidly than many scientists thought possible even a few years ago. There is no political or economic movement presently underway sufficient to stop the process short of a doubling or tripling of the background level of 280 ppm CO_2 in the atmosphere. On the horizon are other threats to humanity and nature in the form of self-replicating technologies, such as nanobots and genetically modified organisms, that may place humankind and natural systems in even greater jeopardy.

2. The forces of denial in the United States are more militant and brazen than ever before. Every day millions in this country alone hear that those concerned about the environment are "wackos" or worse. A former Wyoming senator charges that the environmental movement is "a front for these terrorists" and no significant Washington politician utters any objection.[2] And people holding such opinions have been appointed to strategic positions throughout the federal government.

3. The movement to preserve a habitable planet is caught in the cross fire between fundamentalists of the corporate-dominated global economy and those of atavistic religious movements. It is far easier to see the latter than the former, but in a longer perspective, the devotees of perpetual economic expansion and U.S. military domination of the world will be perceived to be at least as dangerous as are those of a purely religious sort. That danger is now magnified by a new far-right strategic doctrine having the status of national policy that permits the United States to strike preemptively at any country deemed to be an enemy, without resort to international law, morality, common sense, or public debate. In the words of one analyst, this is "a strategy to use American military force to permit the continued offloading onto the rest of the world of the ecological costs of the existing U.S. economy—without any short-

term sacrifices on the part of U.S. capitalism, the U.S. political elite or U.S. voters."[3]

4. Fundamentalists of either kind require dependably loathsome enemies. For Osama bin Laden, the United States and George W. Bush admirably serve that purpose. It is no less true that the foundering presidency of Mr. Bush was revitalized by the activities of Mr. bin Laden and subsequently by the less agreeable attributes of Saddam Hussein. For Rush Limbaugh the enemy are his vile fellow citizens disdained as "liberals." Each is fulfilled and defined by an utterly evil enemy that serves to distract and exonerate.

5. There has been a steep erosion of democracy and civil liberties in the United States, driven by what former president Jimmy Carter describes as "a core group of conservatives who are trying to realize long-pent-up ambitions under the cover of the proclaimed war against terrorism."[4] There is a strong antidemocratic movement on the right wing of American politics that would limit voting rights, reduce access to information, and prevent full disclosure of matters about the conduct of the public business and public control of military affairs.

6. In the 1990s massive amounts of wealth was transferred from the poor and middle classes to the richest. By one estimate "the financial wealth of the top 1% exceeds the combined household financial wealth of the bottom 95%."[5] Much of this transfer of wealth was simply theft. In the California energy "crisis" alone, an estimated $30 billion or more was diverted by those utilities that "gamed" the deregulated electric utility system, effectively defrauding the state and its citizens.

7. For nearly a quarter century, government at all levels has been under constant attack by the extreme right wing with the clear intention of eroding our capacity to forge collective solutions. The assumption is now common that markets are "moral," but that publicly created political solutions are not. The result is a continuation of what a Republican president, Teddy Roosevelt, once

described as "a riot of individualistic materialism, under which complete freedom for the individual . . . turned out in practice to mean perfect freedom for the strong to wrong the weak."[6]

8. The strategy, once revealed by Ronald Reagan's director of the Office of the Budget, David Stockman, has been to cut taxes for corporations and the wealthy and increase military spending thereby creating a severe fiscal crisis that requires cutting expenditures for health, education, mass transit, the environment, and cities.

9. Our problems are systemic in nature and will have to be solved at the system level.

10. There are yet good possibilities to avert the worst of what may lie ahead.

In short, we—by which I mean all of those in the movement to preserve the habitability of the Earth—are failing, and we ought to ask why. The reasons can be found neither in the lack of effort or good intention by thousands of scientists, activists, and concerned citizens, nor in a lack of information, data, logic, and scientific evidence. On these counts the movement has grown impressively, as has the quality and quantity of scientific evidence and rational discourse on which it rests. But we must look more deeply at how this is manifest in the larger arena in which public attitudes are formed and the way in which this influences the conduct of the public business.

We are failing, first, because for twenty years or longer, we have tried to be reasonable on their terms, in the belief that we could persuade the powerful if we only offered enough reason, data, evidence, and logic. We have quantified the decline of species, ecosystems, and now planetary systems in exhaustive detail. We bent over backwards to accommodate the style and intellectual predilections of self-described "conservatives" and those for whom the economy is far more important than the environment, in the belief that politeness and good evidence stated in their terms would win the day. Accordingly, we put the case for the Earth and coming generations in the language of economics, science, and law. With remarkably few exceptions we have been reasonable, erudite, clever, cautiously informative, *and,* relative to the magnitude of the challenges before us, ineffective. We do science, write books, publish articles, develop professional societies, attend conferences, and converse learnedly. But they do politics, take over the courts,[7] control the media, and manipulate the fears and resentments endemic to a rapidly changing society.

The movement to preserve a habitable Earth is in failure mode, too, because it is fractured into different factions, groups, and arcane philosophies. In this respect it has come to resemble the nineteenth-century European socialist movement that became bitterly divided into warring factions, each more eager to be right than right and effective. When the world was finally ready for better ideas about how to decently organize industrial society, that movement delivered bolshevism, and the rest, as they say, is history. The left historically has exhausted itself in bloody internecine quarrels, the strategy, as David Brower once described it, of drawing the wagons into a circle and shooting inward. The right generally suffers no such fracturing, in large part because their agenda is formed around less complicated aims having to do with pecuniary advantage.

Jack Turner, too, is right in saying that the movement is in failure mode because all too often it is complacent and lacks passion. "We are," in his words, "a nation of environmental cowards ... willing to accept substitutes, imitations, semblances, and fakes—a diminished wild. We accept abstract information in place of personal experience and communication."[8] Effective protest, he continues, "is grounded in anger and we are not (consciously) angry. Anger nourishes hope and fuels rebellion, it presumes a judgment, presumes how things ought to be and aren't, presumes a caring. Emotion remains the best evidence of belief and value. Unfortunately, there is little connection between our emotions and the wild."[9] We are endlessly busy trading e-mails, doing research, writing papers, and attending conferences in exotic places but go into the wild less and less often. We are cut off from the source.

Finally, we are losing because we have failed to appreciate the depth of human needs for transcendence and belonging. We have allowed those intending to pillage the last of nature to do so behind the cover of religion, national pride, community, and family. As a result, the majority of U.S. citizens—even those who regard themselves as "environmentalists"—see little conflict with the goals of human domination of nature and the perpetual expansion of the human estate on Earth. But whatever we thought we were doing, the system we have built is based on illusion, greed, and ill will disguised by patriotism, religious doctrine, and individualism.

What is to be done? To that question there can be no simple, easy, or definitive answer, but I do think there are some obvious places to begin. The first requires that we take back public words such as "conservative" and "patriot," which have been co-opted and put to no good or accurate use. How is it, for example, that the word "conservative" is used to describe those willing to run irreversible risks with the Earth? Intending to conserve nothing, they are not conservatives at all but vandals now working at a global scale. How have those driving their sport utility vehicles to the mall, sporting two American flags and a "God bless America" bumper sticker come to regard themselves as patriots? They are not authentic patriots but merely self-indulgent. As noted in chapter one, the great and noble word "liberal" has been demeaned and slandered. How have we allowed that to happen? Unable to defend the integrity of words, we cannot defend the Earth or anything else.

The integrity of our common language, however, depends a great deal on the cultivation of discerning intelligence in the public and that requires better education than we now have. But education has been whittled down to smaller purposes of passing tests and ensuring large "lifetime earnings" in some part of the global economy. What passes for education has become highly technical and specialized, little of which is aimed to draw out the full human stature of young people. We've become a nation of specialists and technicians, not broadly educated and discerning people. Scholars have been too intent on developing "professional knowledge," arcane theories, and complicated methodologies, instead of broad knowledge useful to the wider public. Consequently, we have fewer and fewer people who know history, or how the world works as a physical system, or the rudiments of the Constitution, or who have a logical political philosophy. We are a people ripe for the plucking.

This leads to another point. We do not have an environmental crisis so much as we have a political crisis. A great majority of people still wish a decent and habitable world for their descendants, but those desires are thwarted by the machinery that ought to connect the popular will to public decisions but no longer does so. We will have to repair and perhaps reinvent the institutions of democratic governance for a global world, and that means dealing with issues that the founders of this republic did not and could not have anticipated. The process of political engagement at all levels has become increasingly confusing, and inaccessible. And in the mass consumption society we have all become better consumers than citizens, which is to say, willing participants in our own undoing. The solution, however difficult, is to reconnect people with the political process and government at all levels.

It is also necessary to expose the mythology that surrounds what Marjorie Kelly calls "the divine rights of capital" and place democratic controls on corporations and the movement of capital.[10] We once fought a revolutionary war to establish political democracy in western societies, but have yet to democratize the workplace and the ownership of capital. These are still governed by the same illogic of unquestioned divine right by which monarchies once ruled. The assumption that corporations are legal persons and thereby granted rights of privacy that place them beyond effective public scrutiny, control, and, often, law is foolishness and worse. The latest corporate scandals are only that: the latest in a recurring pattern of illegality, self-dealing, and political corruption surpassing even that of the robber baron era. The solution is to enforce corporate charters as a public license to do business on behalf of the public and to make them revocable if and when the terms of the charter are violated. If private ownership of capital is a good thing, it should be widely extended, not restricted to the wealthy. By the same logic, we must remove the corrupting influence of money from politics beginning with corporate campaign contributions and the hundreds of billions of dollars of public subsidies for cars, highways, fossil fuels, and nuclear power that corrupt the democratic process and public policy.

Political reform requires an active, engaged, and sometimes enraged citizenry. Compare, for example, the Illinois farmer-citizens who stood for hours to hear Lincoln and Douglas debate issues of slavery and sectionalism in 1858. Those debates were full of careful argument, eloquence, and wit. Those citizens applauded, laughed, and jeered, which is to say that they followed the flow of argument and heard what was being said. Later, some died for and because of those same arguments. They were citizens and were willing to sacrifice a great deal for that privilege. In our time, while the issues have grown to global scale with consequences that extend as far into the future as the mind dares to imagine, political argument is whittled down to sound bytes squeezed between advertisements. The means by which citizens are informed have been increasingly monopolized and manipulated. Only half or less of the citizenry bothers to vote. Some believe public apathy and political incompetence to be good or at least tolerable. I do not. Unless we reverse course they will, in time, prove to be the undoing of democratic government and all that depends on a healthy democracy. The nature of what will replace it is already evident: an unconstrained managerial and well-armed plutocracy intent on global plunder.

The environmental movement needs a positive strategy

that fires the public imagination. The public, I think, knows what we are against, but not what we are for. There are many things that should be stopped, but what should be started? The answer to that question lies in a more coherent agenda formed around what is being called ecological design as it applies to land use, buildings, energy systems, transportation, materials, water, agriculture, forestry, and urban planning. For three decades and longer we have been developing the ideas, science, and technological wherewithal to build a sustainable society. The public knows of these things only in fragments, but not as a coherent and practical agenda—indeed the only practical course available. That is our fault and we should start now to put a positive agenda before the public that includes the human and economic advantages of better technology, integrated planning, coherent purposes, and foresight.

Finally, all of us should expect far more of leaders than we presently do. Never has the need for genuine leadership been greater, and seldom has it been less evident. We cannot be ruled by ignorant, malicious, greedy, incompetent, and shortsighted people and expect things to turn out well. If we are to navigate the challenges of the decades ahead, what E. O. Wilson calls "the bottleneck," we will need leaders of great stature, clarity of mind, spiritual depth, courage, and vision. We need leaders who see patterns that connect us across the divisions of culture, religion, geography, and time. We need leadership that draws us together to resolve conflicts, move quickly from fossil fuels to solar power, reverse global environmental deterioration, and empower us to provide shelter, food, medical care, decent livelihood, and education for everyone. We need leadership that is capable of energizing genuine commitment to old and venerable traditions as well as new visions for a global civilization that preserves and honors local cultures, economies, and knowledge. And we need leaders with the kind of humility demonstrated by Czech president Vaclav Havel:

In time I have become a good deal less sure of myself, a good deal more humble . . . every day I suffer more and more from stage fright; every day I am more afraid that I won't be up to the job . . . more and more often, I am afraid that I will fall woefully short of expectations, that I will somehow reveal my own lack of qualifications for the job, that despite my good faith I will make ever greater mistakes, that I will cease to be trustworthy and therefore lose the right to do what I do.[11]

Rewriting the Ten Commandments

> I was nakedly cruel toward Dukakis. And I am sorry. . . . My illness helped me see that what was missing in society is what was missing in me. A little heart, a lot of brotherhood.
>
> —LEE ATWATER

But it took a fatal illness for Lee Atwater to become an advocate of brotherhood. Earlier in his career as the coordinator of George H. W. Bush's 1988 presidential campaign, chairman of the Republican Party, and mentor to Carl Rove, he perfected the pit-bull tactics that have become the Ten Commandments of American politics. After the election of 2000 the two-party system is now fractured into warring camps, while the presidency and Supreme Court have lost a great deal of their former legitimacy. Democracies are always fragile systems, vulnerable to breakdown of civility, rules, and tolerance. Politics in American history have seldom been known for high mindedness, but not since the middle of the nineteenth century have they been as bitter as they are at present. And it could not have come at a worse time. At the very time that we need to be taking farsighted steps to curtail greenhouse gas emissions, protect ecosystems, conserve biological diversity, and move the world toward a decent future, we are locked in denial. In the meantime critical thresholds are going by like mile markers on a highway and with every marker passed, good possibilities ratchet downward.

Whatever hope we have of changing course now depends on understanding the prevailing political rules, not to emulate them, but to change them. The rules that must be changed are these:

1. Appeal always to peoples' resentments and fears, not to their rationality, compassion, or farsightedness.
2. Confuse, obfuscate, and muddy the waters, never clarify or instruct particularly on issues of long-term importance. Do not ask the public to understand complex issues. And never ask the public to sacrifice even for the sake of their children's future. Remember, as George H. W. Bush put it in 1992, the "American way of life is not negotiable" even when it is wasteful, inefficient, unfair, and counterproductive.
3. Demonize your opponents and promise to restore honor and "character," implying that the other side has neither.
4. Investigate your adversaries without ceasing. People will assume that anyone under investigation must be guilty of something.
5. Applaud scientific evidence when it supports corporate profits, oppose it when it has to do with human health, biotic impoverishment, and climate change.
6. Politicize everything, particularly the courts.
7. Have no enemies to the right, no matter how outrageous or mistaken they may be.
8. Appease the religious right at all costs. And, if you can manage it, claim to be born again. Never give details.
9. Protect and expand corporate power and the interests of short-term wealth while attacking government as the sole source of all problems.

10. And of course, insist that the other side stop "partisan bickering."]

These are the rules for a scorched earth, take no prisoners kind of politics. And they are leaving behind political ruin and crippling our capacity for the kind of broad consensual political action we will have to take soon if we are to avoid the worst of what looms ahead. This is the politics of cynicism, aimed to undermine robust democracy in which all people, their votes and their lives, really do count, and to do so by what appear to be democratic means. This kind of politics works as long as there is a spineless, perhaps mendacious, media to put the right "spin" on things.

[The collapse of communism and the absence of dependably loathsome enemies confounded the right wing in American politics for a time. But Rush Limbaugh, Newt Gingrich, Tom DeLay, Grover Norquist, Karl Rove, Trent Lott, and other warriors of the right discovered the new threat posed by "liberals," minorities, women, gays, and environmentalists. The right wing in American politics has always needed enemies, even when it had to invent them. Its national legacy, among other things, includes McCarthyism, Watergate, the Iran-Contra scandal, record deficits, government shutdown, impeachment of a president they could not defeat at the polls, and an electoral coup d'etat orchestrated between the governor of Florida, Florida state officials, and Republicans in the Florida legislature, the U.S. Congress, and the Supreme Court. The local legacy of right-wing politics is, in too many places, a kind of look the other way approach that condones hate crimes, proliferation of deadly weaponry, the growth of militias, and a mountain of hypocrisy.]

None of this exonerates the Democrats and moderates of either party. They are complicit in the corruption of our democracy. With a few exceptions like the late Paul Wellstone, they have been lukewarm and uninspired advocates for the poor, children, the working class, future generations, endangered species, forests, and ecosystems. It is time to reexamine American democracy and its prospects.

In one of the most prescient books of the twentieth century, historian Walter Prescott Webb argued that democracy became possible after 1500 when the ratios of population to land and resources expanded with the discovery of the New World. In his words, "these boom-born institutions, economic systems, political systems, social systems—in short, the present superstructure of Western civilization—are today founded on boom conditions."[1] Ours, he wrote, is "an abnormal age, and not a progressive orderly development which mankind was destined to make anyway." Capitalism and democracy were both "subsidized" by the frontier "in a way we seldom admit."[2] During the course of the twentieth century, all the ratios of population to land and resources returned to where they had been in Europe in the year 1500.

Democracy in Webb's view was an artifact of abundance, but a large fraction of that abundance has been used up by the boom economy. Our demands have now outstripped the surplus provided by nature. What we count as prosperity now depends heavily on drawing down natural capital of soils, biological diversity, forests, and climatic stability. What remains must be stretched over the needs, aspirations, and wants of 6.3 billion people—a number that will rise to 8–11 billion in this century. We are simply not as rich as we presume.

How will democracy survive with several billion people severely impoverished in a world full of ethnic hatreds and coming apart because of growing stresses of rapid climatic change, soil loss, and the breakdown of entire ecosystems? How will it survive in a United States divided between gated communities and decaying inner cities? How will it survive the erosion of community and a public increasingly unhinged from reality by a pervasive entertainment culture?

Robert Kaplan once asked whether "democracy [was] just a moment," not an inevitable historical trend. There are important thinkers who believe it will be just that. After surveying our prospects, economist Robert Heilbroner once wrote that "I not only predict but I prescribe a centralization of power as the only means by which our threatened and dangerous civilization will make way for its successor."[3] Political scientist William Ophuls similarly argued that without "a population willing and able to restrain its own appetites for the sake of the common good . . . ecological scarcity [will] engender overwhelming pressures toward political systems that are frankly authoritarian by current standards."[4] That kind of restraint, however, does not have a chance in a society marinating in hypermaterialism and so, perhaps, we do indeed face more dire possibilities. But far from some kind of ecological authoritarianism, we are witnessing the opposite: authoritarianism imposed by corporate interests—what E. L. Doctorow calls the "eighth circle of thieves" whose goal is to keep the present system going as long as possible, whatever it takes. These are the oilmen, the coal men, purveyors of sprawl, advertisers, and the folks who profit greatly from building roads and automobiles.

It would be a mistake to dismiss these and their allies as stupid people. Some may be mired deep in denial and ignorance, but I think many of them know the score. For those that do, the logic of political economy goes something like this:

- An economy that does not grow will die, so growth must continue at all costs;
- Without growth, redistribution of wealth would be necessary;
- Redistribution, however, would encourage social decay and invite social chaos—to say nothing about its effects on the privileges of the wealthy;
- Economic growth, therefore, is the only way to maintain social cohesion;
- Conservation is unsuited to a growth economy, hence;
- Growth requires unlimited access to fossil energy, forest products, and minerals that are becoming more scarce in the United States;

- Unimpeded access to global markets will make up for the depletion of U.S. resources; and
- Military power, including the control of space, is essential to maintain access to resources worldwide.]

This is the logic of the powerful and comfortable, much taken with the philosophy of after us, the deluge. Like Dostoyevsky's Grand Inquisitor, they fashion themselves as imminently practical and regard the general public as sheep. Present appearances notwithstanding, their power and influence is as vulnerable as that of the managers of the Soviet Union in the 1980s. They intend merely to buy as much time as realpolitik can purchase in order to hog as much as can be hogged in the remaining years before it all goes bust. Some certainly know that the big numbers are moving inexorably against them and will, in the not-too-distant future, bury them. The problem is that the resulting collapse will bury the rest of us as well.

Such politics are utterly inappropriate for the challenges of the twenty-first century—what Thomas Berry calls the "Great Work." Our task is to begin "the transition from a period of human devastation of the Earth to a period when humans would [relate] to the planet in a mutually beneficial manner."[5] The Great Work requires us, among other things, to make a rapid transition from

- Fossil fuels to renewable energy sources,
- An extractive to a regenerative economy patterned on natural systems,
- Inequity within and between generations to fairness, and from
- Violence toward people and nature to nonviolence.

The challenge of the Great Work is nothing less than a moral and ecological recalibration of humans in the biosphere. We did not chose this work any more than the generation of World War II chose to fight Nazism or that of the 1860s chose to fight slavery. But it is our challenge and we must rise to it. It is like no other challenge humankind has ever faced. And it will require—if we make it—a transition in virtually every aspect of our material and political life.

But the challenge of the Great Work is first and foremost one to our spirit, and for that we need, not authoritarian government, but a better and wiser kind of politics. As Czech president Vaclav Havel describes it,

> Genuine politics—politics worthy of the name, and the only politics I am willing to devote myself to—is simply a matter of serving those around us: serving the community, and serving those who will come after us. Its deepest roots are moral because it is a responsibility, expressed through action, to and for the whole, a responsibility that is what it is—a "higher" responsibility—only because it has a metaphysical grounding: that is it grows out of a conscious or subconscious certainty that our death ends nothing, because everything is forever being recorded and evaluated somewhere else, somewhere "above us," in what I have called "the memory of being."[6]

If we want a better world than that now in prospect "we must—as humanity, as people, as conscious beings with spirit, mind, and a sense of responsibility—somehow come to our senses."[7]

Coming to our senses politically will mean transcending both right-wing fanaticism and "market madness" and the left-wing illusions and utopias.[8] Far from discarding democracy, it will mean readapting it to meet the radically different conditions of the twenty-first century. It will mean rethinking old assumptions about the conduct of public business for and by business. A genuine politics would not assume that corporations have the same rights as persons, or that wealth buys special privilege.[9] Instead of unaccountable global hierarchies, a genuine politics would be formed on robust local institutions and strong communities. The processes of genuine politics would help to form an authentic public engaged in the conduct of public affairs. It would elevate the public mind, not pander to the lowest common denominator. It would promote the general interest, not particular interests. It would raise standards of fairness. A genuine politics would not have to be gussied up to appeal to one religious group or another. And a genuine politics would not permit the interests of its children to be discounted for any reason whatsoever.

Genuine politics would require genuine leaders, people of full stature equipped to do the hard work of educating the public, rebuilding political institutions fallen into disrepair, and refocusing our attention on the Great Work ahead. Authentic leadership cannot be bought. It does not cater to our wants, but calls us to do our duty. Real leaders inspire, energize, and motivate us to be better and wiser citizens than we would otherwise be. The irony of great leadership is that it inspires leadership at all levels. And if we are not to surrender to authoritarian temptations of either left or right we must become competent and diligent citizens making communities that work in the fullest sense of the word.

Make no mistake, the work ahead will be hard, but easier by far than not doing it. Authentic leaders of the twenty-first century will help us understand that to continue our present course is sheer madness. They will help to chart the transition from the cowboy economy powered by fossil fuels to a world powered by sunlight. They will help to redefine prosperity from that dependent on robbing our children to one that protects soils, forests, biological diversity, ecological resilience, and entire ecosystems for our children. Above all, real leaders will help us rewrite the rules for the conduct of our public business to read like this:

- Appeal to voters' rationality, compassion, and vision
- Instruct, clarify, elevate the political dialogue
- Honor your adversaries—politics ought not to be a war, but a conversation
- Find common ground
- Never corrupt, politicize, or ignore scientific evidence
- Maintain the separation of executive, legislative, and judicial power

- Hold your own side to rigorous standards of fairness and decency
- Maintain the separation of religion and state
- Insist on the same kind of separation between money and politics
- Be willing to risk losing elections for the right reasons.

What sounds so idealistic—the improvement of our politics—is the only realistic hope we have to surmount the challenges ahead. In practical terms this will mean not merely reforming the way we finance elections, but throwing private money out of the electoral process altogether. It will mean reclaiming words like "patriotism" that have been appropriated by zealots. And it will mean rebuilding civic competence and the public capacity to solve public problems. Perhaps the greatest irony of our time is that what once appeared to be altruism is, in fact, the foundation for a higher form of self-interest based on the inescapable fact that our prospects are now joined. To the skeptics, I would say we've risen to the challenges before and we must do it again.

At the end of his life Lee Atwater had it right. And getting it right, in Vaclav Havel's words, means, "If there is to be any chance at all of success, there is only one way to strive for decency, reason, responsibility, sincerity, civility, and tolerance, and that is decently, reasonably, responsibly, sincerely, civilly, and tolerantly."[10]

five

The Events of 9/11:
A View from the Margin

> Fanaticism consists in redoubling your efforts when you have forgotten your aim.
> —GEORGE SANTAYANA

Immediately after the terrorist attacks in New York and Washington, George W. Bush labeled the events "an act of war," not an international crime, and proceeded to invade two countries, threaten others deemed to be "evil," and claim the right to preemptively strike any other country alleged to support terrorism or presuming to challenge U.S. military domination. With considerably less fanfare he also eviscerated the enforcement of environmental laws and defunded social programs. The strategy was to proceed by stealth past a frightened and distracted public. A Congress dominated by the right wing of the Republican Party, for its part, suspended significant parts of our civil liberties and stood ready to further impair Bill of Rights protections in the aftermath of any future terrorist attack.

There can be no question that those guilty of committing atrocities deserve to be apprehended and punished or that terrorism poses a serious threat to the United States, but the war on terrorism has been used to push a far-right agenda under the guise of security. That much is clear, but little else is. This is a good time to reassess the underlying structure of political discontent that leads to terrorism, the vulnerability of modern societies, global poverty, and the relationship between these things and a deteriorating global environment.

Why do so many around the world hate Americans? Why is the United States so vulnerable to terrorism? Most important, what can be done to break the cycle of violence and lay the foundation for real global security? The answers, whatever they may be, require that we place the events of 9/11 into a more thoughtful context than "evil people attacked us with no cause."

First, it is clear that the acts of 9/11 were remarkably cost-effective. For no more than a few hundred thousand dollars, the perpetrators used our equipment and facilities to cause hundreds of billions of dollars of damage and seize control of Western media for months. They imposed a tax of billions more to pay for remedial actions and subsequent economic losses. We know that more devastating options throughout the United States, Europe, and Japan are available to determined terrorists and to the merely deranged. The next round could involve suitcase nuclear weapons, chemical or biological materials, cyberterrorism, or just the sabotage of basic services, communications networks, roads, bridges, and industrial infrastructure. In such cases high-technology weapons are worse than useless. They create a false sense of security at a huge expense while preempting smarter options that promote real security.

From conflicts in Northern Ireland, the Balkans, the Middle East, and dozens of other places we know that there are points of no return where memory becomes myth, martyrs are deified, enemies demonized, positions harden into bitterness, and disputes become perpetual. Inevitably, the political discussion narrows in ways that prevent long-term solutions to the underlying problems that created the conflict in the first place. Human affairs have their own laws of action and reaction that displace logic, reason, and justice, which is to say that it is probable that a response in kind will trigger further violence. In such situations there is no possible victory for either side . . . ever.

Any effective response to terrorism requires that we comprehend, too, the larger context beginning with the fact that the global economy has become highly stratified with a small number of very wealthy at the top and several billions, including some who will become terrorists, living in extreme poverty. We know that the United States is the world's largest vendor of weapons and that Osama bin Laden and Saddam Hussein once received U.S. support and financing. For fifty years the United States engaged in political manipulation, trained and financed death squads, and funded repressive dictatorships. It has, thereby, contributed to a global pattern of violence and hostility that is not improved by the fact that the present U.S. administration has chosen to ignore, violate, or abrogate international agreements about climatic change, arms control, and chemical/biological weapons while now demanding international cooperation in Iraq. The United States cannot have it both ways. Either it is part of a global community or must act alone. If the latter, it will lose and lose tragically even if it can "win" a war with a particular terrorist or country.

Finally, we have created a tightly coupled world in which ecological, economic, political, and technological effects of actions anywhere sooner or later touch everyone. It is a world vulnerable to disruption from a thousand sources. It cannot be sustained politically or ecologically. For all of the hype about freedom, the emerging world system is neither very free nor very democratic. It is, rather, being driven by a plutocracy of distant and unaccountable corporations, global agencies like the World Trade Organization, and compliant governments. But in the end it is a world ruled by ironies of the sort that what goes around, comes around. The United States aimed to be rich and powerful, but has succeeded in making itself a very large bull's-eye, more vulnerable and despised than most Americans care to admit.

The events of 9/11, in short, dramatically underscored the clash between two kinds of fanaticism. On one side are those wishing to stop all change and freeze societies into extreme male-dominated and violence-prone theocracies ruled by the likes of the Taliban. On the other, are the free-market fundamentalists who intend to change everything for everyone, everywhere, all the time. The one is a rearguard protest against the modern world and Westernization in particular. The other is a global juggernaut driven by financial markets, technological dynamism, global capitalism, and the temptation to use high-tech weapons. It is easy to see the insanity in the former. But in more reflective times the latter, perhaps, will be seen as the more sweeping kind of derangement. In the no-man's-land between the acolytes of two fundamentalisms, good possibilities can be lost, and the possibility of building a just world society that can be sustained ecologically could recede into the background, making for a future ruled by fear, vengeance, and reprisal. If we are not to acquiesce to that dark future, we must reexamine old myths about globalization, economic growth, and national security.

What do those of us in the conservation community have to offer to that effort? What powerful and unifying ideas do we have that might clarify the situation and help forge better policy? Failing to announce better possibilities we risk becoming irrelevant in an increasingly militarized world divided into garrison states, fundamentalist sects, terrorist cells, drug lords with their armies and addicts, and global corporations with theirs.

We should not be silent. We urgently need a more coherent and accurate view of the world as the foundation for more effective and humane governance and smarter solutions to seemingly intractable problems. Effective political action requires, in Wendell Berry's felicitous words, "solving for [a] pattern" that is now global. There is no good way to separate policies for the economy, trade, energy, and security from those affecting land use, climate, forests, soils, and communities. But to unify these requires the willingness to see connections and the ability to comprehend how a complex global system works. Eventually all actions of governments, including those to promote economic development and national security, affect natural systems and biogeochemical cycles, either compounding our problems or resolving them at a higher level.

In an ecological perspective, in other words, there are few accidents or anomalies, only outcomes based on system structure and dynamics. Climate change and glittering malls, Calcuttan poverty and sybaritic wealth, biotic impoverishment and economic growth, militarism and terrorism, global domination and utter vulnerability are not different things but manifestations of a single system.

The world community faces growing conflicts over access to freshwater, declining oceanic fisheries, climatic change, access to oil, and the mounting effects of the loss of natural capital. The challenges of global poverty, feeding another one to three billion people, arresting climatic change, preserving biotic diversity, *and* maintaining world peace will become more and more difficult especially given the spread of the means of violence. In the twenty-first century no nation on its own can be secure and no narrow definition of security will provide a foundation for safety. The idea of security must be broadened to include security against hunger, pollution, ecological degradation, poverty, ignorance, *and* direct physical assaults for everyone. Anything less will not work for long. Meeting human needs for food, shelter, sustainable livelihood, and environmental preservation reduces the sources of conflict and the dissatisfaction that feeds terrorism. Real security will require a larger vision and the development of the international capacity necessary to solve problems that feed violence, hatred, and fear.

An ecological perspective could help to dramatically

decrease our vulnerability. The way we provision ourselves with food, energy, materials, and water increases or decreases our vulnerability to system failures, terrorists, acts of God, and ecological degradation. A society with many nuclear reactors is vulnerable in ways that one powered by decentralized solar technologies is not. Similarly, a society fed by a few megafarms is far more vulnerable to many kinds of disruption than one with many relatively smaller and widely dispersed farms. One that relies on long-distance transport of essential materials must guard every supply line, but the military capability to do so becomes yet another source of vulnerability and ecological cost. In short, no society that relies on distant sources of food, energy, and materials or heroic feats of technology can be secured indefinitely. An ecological view would suggest more resilient and cost-effective ways to provision ourselves that create fewer targets for terrorists while buffering us from other sources of disruption. An ecological view of security would lead us to rebuild family farms, local enterprises, community prosperity, regional economies, and invest in the regeneration of natural capital. And we know how to design and build energy efficient buildings, utilize current solar income, farm sustainably, rebuild greener cities, and manage resources for the long-term. The challenge is not know-how but one of political will and leadership.

I furthermore believe that we can help expose the lie in the assertion by George H. W. Bush that "the American way of life is not negotiable." No way of life based on inequity, waste, economic exploitation, military coercion, and a refusal to account all costs is non-negotiable. Terrorists on 9/11 unilaterally negotiated the American way of life downward by several trillion dollars and they could continue to do so. The question before the United States is not whether we can maintain a way of life based on imported oil and resources, great environmental damage, and climatic change. We cannot. Rather the question is whether we can summon the intelligence and wit to create a just, secure, and sustainable prosperity that no terrorist can threaten and that threatens no other nation. The ecological and security costs of military power are high and growing. But real security is more complicated and a great deal cheaper. It has to do with the connections between the health of democratic institutions, the fair distribution of wealth, military power, *and* the protection of soils, forests, and biological diversity. There would be no better first step to ensure our security and that of others than a resolute decision that we will end our dependence on foreign oil—and all fossil fuels—by tapping technological ingenuity to increase our energy efficiency, harness renewable energy, and build a more resilient, less centralized energy system.[1] Thereafter our engagement in the politics of an unstable region might be by choice, not permanent necessity. In the meantime we would have lowered our balance of payments deficit, reduced air pollution, created many new jobs along with the technological basis for a solar-hydrogen economy, reduced the emission of greenhouse gases, and dramatically lessened our vulnerability.

The Labors of Sisyphus

Danish professor Bjorn Lomborg's book, *The Skeptical Environmentalist*, caused a stir when it first appeared in the fall of 2001. On its cover the book was hailed as a "brilliant and powerful" expose of "appalling errors" committed by environmentalists. Unsurprisingly, it was reported to be a favorite of Vice President Dick Cheney, not otherwise noted for the quality or range of his reading habits. It is in the genre of criticism of Julian Simon and indeed the author attributes his position to reading an interview with Simon in *Wired Magazine* in 1997, after which this self-described "old left-wing Greenpeace member" was never the same. As a result he set off on a debunking expedition through an unexplored continent of environmental error and exaggeration. On his return, Lomborg was greeted by some at dockside as a latter-day Christopher Columbus. He received cheery accolades from the *Economist*, including a two-page excerpt from the book and one extraordinarily kind review that noted the author's telegenic potential as a further reason to take his mere ideas seriously. Whatever the merits in that position, the financial media and anti-environmentalists generally have been much impressed and fortified by Lomborg's skepticism.

On closer inspection *The Skeptical Environmentalist* is edifying but perhaps not quite in the way its author intended. I hasten to say that skepticism is an admirable quality of mind especially when disciplined by honesty, clarity, and knowledge adequate to the subject. The book should not be dismissed because its message may discomfit those who believe the global environment, on balance, to be in decline. Having said that, it's instructive to note the form, volume, and substance of Mr. Lomborg's kind of skepticism in order that we might improve our understanding of environmental issues and trends and the controversies these provoke.

Lomborg's skepticism is sizeable. The book is 515 double-columned large pages with small print. It has 173 figures and 2,930 much-touted footnotes, many from comforting sources. The table of contents includes issues of human welfare, life expectancy, food/hunger, prosperity, forests, energy, resources, water, air pollution, acid rain, water pollution, space, chemicals, biodiversity, and global warming. It is a tome. In the five years or so since his conversion Lomborg has attempted to master a great deal. The result is overwhelming in terms of sheer bulk among other things.

Lomborg, a statistician, intends to slay errors indigenous to environmentalism with numbers and the book offers a great many that purport to contradict prevailing scientific and environmental belief. He announces early on that "I am not myself an expert as regards environmental problems."[1] We may take him at his word, and in the spirit of skepticism we may be justifiably wary of his numbers and the use he makes of them.

The point of *The Skeptical Environmentalist* is straightforward. At the beginning the author announces that he "care[s] for our Earth" but wants us not to act on myth in the service of reaching a "better tomorrow."[2] Fair enough. He then proceeds to describe what he calls "the Litany," a long list of environmental problems, issues, and analysis. He does not like the work of the Worldwatch Institute and any number of other environmental organizations. They feed a media that "cannot survive without an audience" most easily gotten by featuring "bad news."[3] "Our fear," Lomborg concludes, "is due to . . . the fact that we are given ever more negative information by scientists, the organizations and the media."[4] Etcetera. Alas, "the Litany" turns out to be a "Great Fable" foisted on the public by the likes of Lester Brown, Paul Ehrlich, Al Gore, the World-watch Institute, Greenpeace, and such. What Lomborg calls "The Real State of the World" is quite good: "the last 400 years brought us fantastic and continued progress"; "all indicators of human welfare show improvement"; "we are not overexploiting our renewable resources"; "human health has benefited phenomenally"; "tomorrow's problems" of toxics, loss of biodiversity, and climate change, are merely solvable problems, and "we know of no other substantial problems looming on the horizon."[5] The human record is one of unbroken progress and much more is in sight; "the world is basically headed in the right direction."[6]

To refute "the Litany" having to do with problems of carrying capacity, ecological resilience, loss of biodiversity, and climate change Lomborg offers many contrary numbers. But what can be said about the quality of his data and analysis? Knowledgeable reviewers note that he uses data selectively and often inaccurately; his grasp of science is tenuous; his treatment of complex issues is superficial and frequently misleading. Writing in *Science,* Michael Grubb of Imperial College (London) notes that Lomborg "generally pays inadequate attention to serious environmental problems in developing countries" and that he displays "a stunning lack of attention to cause and effect."[7] Further, "he shows no appreciation for the practical or the moral dimensions of impacts on potentially billions of people."[8] Lomborg's characterization of the work of the Intergovernmental Panel on Climatic Change is marred by "significant distortions," offers "nothing new or insightful," and reflects "ignorance of the Kyoto Protocol and of the underlying economic and political debates."[9]

Similarly, regarding the loss of species, Thomas Lovejoy

notes that Lomborg confuses the "process of extinction by which a species is judged to be extinct with the estimates and projections of extinction rates."[10] Lomborg's analysis has a kind of "Alice-in-Wonderland" quality reflecting a "pattern of denial," "errors of bias," "careless mistakes," and an "ignorance of how environmental science proceeds."[11]

In the views of its critics *The Skeptical Environmentalist*, disguised beneath a blizzard of footnotes and charts, is a polemic and not an evenhanded effort to accurately "measure the true state of the planet" as the subtitle promises. There are enough serious factual errors and distortions that Lomborg will be widely dismissed by the majority of those who study these issues for a living. Indeed, the Danish Research Agency's Committee on Scientific Dishonesty concluded that the book is "scientifically dishonest."[12] On the other hand, Lomborg will be much praised, if seldom read, by those whose living depends much on preserving the status quo.

Beyond disputes of fact and analysis, *The Skeptical Environmentalist* raises more substantial issues of the kind once described by Austrian Harvard economist Joseph Schumpeter as "pre-analytic assumptions." These are mostly unstated and unexamined beliefs that influence and sometimes determine how we see the world and select data to support hidden predispositions. Early on, for example, Lomborg announces that "the only scarce good is money with which to solve problems."[13] Despite a subsequent demurral that "I am [not] a demonic little free-market individualist," it is clear that he adopts the market as described and defended by mainstream neoclassical economists as the final arbiter of the public good.[14] He does so, however, without acknowledging that large subsidies distort supposedly "free" markets or that market prices seldom reflect the true costs of consumption. As a result, his economic analysis is highly misleading. He asserts, for example, that "only when we get sufficiently rich can we afford the relative luxury of caring about the environment,"[15] without noting the strong correlation between increasing wealth of a society and its impact on climate, species loss, and use of toxics long acknowledged by alert economists.[16]

Likewise, Lomborg concludes that global warming "will cost us approximately 0.5 percent of our overall consumption . . . and is not anywhere near the most important problem facing the world."[17] He therefore concludes that the money necessary to implement the Kyoto Protocol would be better spent to help the poor in the third world.[18] Lomborg goes on to attack the Kyoto Protocol as inadequate. He is right to do so. But instead of arguing for a more adequate response to climatic change, he dismisses much of the scientific evidence about the potential severity of the problem and consigns its resolution to the market rigged to expand the fossil-fuel-powered consumer economy on the faith that economic growth will solve all problems.

The absence of the words "democracy" and "corporation" in the index and his 2,930 footnotes says a great deal about Lomborg's worldview. Since government policy and citizen action do not count for much, he reaches conclusions that do not square with history. Air pollution in London, for example, is magically cleaned by the invisible hand of the market, not by public action. He makes no mention of the 1956 Clean Air Act that banned coal burning over much of London.[19] Lomborg's is a world without politics, democracy, citizens, and a public. It has only consumers and markets. Yet much if not most of the environmental improvements he notices have been due to specific policies and laws that were driven by public concerns and implemented by elected governments. Much of the improvement he notes is otherwise inexplicable.

Further, the author's world is one without surprises, thresholds, points of no return, negative synergies, and irreversibility. There are no places where angels fear to tread. Looking ahead, Lomborg sees nothing but solvable and relatively minor problems, never irony, paradox, or dilemmas. The complexities of ecology or the dynamics of complex human/ecological systems disappear. Forests are good mostly for producing commercial products and providing recreation.[20] Their more diverse and complex ecological services go unmentioned. "The green revolution," he confidently states, "represents a milestone in the history of mankind" providing a "fantastic increase in food production."[21] He makes no mention of its environmental or social costs, dependence on cheap fossil fuels, or the alternative potential to make agriculture sustainable by mimicking natural systems.

The result is a level of almost euphoric optimism that allows Lomborg to assert that "today's world is much less vulnerable, precisely because trade and transport effectively act to reduce local risks."[22] The ecological/social catastrophes like those in Rwanda, the Sudan, Ethiopia, and the Dominican Republic disappear. So too, the negative effects of free trade, the causes of terrorism, and the moral/political complexities of technological choices. The author can see no way that global civilization might come tumbling down like a house of cards, and consequently he can see no reason to advocate that we hedge our bets, take out insurance, or act with precaution. To the contrary, he dismisses what he calls "the insurance mentality" held "by those who harbor an intense dislike of risk-taking."[23] Lomborg does not say anything about the difference between small and voluntary risks like the decision to smoke compared to those that are planetwide, imposed by a small number of elites, and irreversible. Nor does he say who has the right to make such decisions and on what basis, let alone who benefits and who pays. Such questions do not fit easily into graphs and statistics.

Lomborg and his defenders are hard pressed to explain the sizeable discrepancy between the conclusions reached in *The Skeptical Environmentalist* and those of the vast majority of environmental scientists, environmental advocates, and well-read scholars. Predictably, the explanation given is that the media "prefer[s] pessimism," that environmentalists offer a great deal of it and "scientists have vested interests in pessimism. The study of global warming has brought them fame, funds, speaking fees and room service."[24] Oddly, in a book advertised as a veritable fountain of empirical evidence, none is offered to support that allegation. On the other hand Lomborg and his defenders ignore the well-documented funding from the fossil fuel industry that supports the few global warming skeptics he cites as authorities in the subject.[25]

Like the labors of Sisyphus, environmental scientists are condemned regularly to roll the rock of public awareness and comprehension back up the mountain. But it does not stay there for long. A Simon, or Easterbrook, or Lomborg, or any number of corporate advertising agents or their lobbyists, or befuddled politicians come along regularly to kick it off again. It is much easier to make intellectual messes than it is to clarify complicated issues, especially when real solutions would challenge the status quo and require much careful thought across many fields of knowledge. Problems of climatic change, biotic impoverishment, population growth, and the choices to be made about various technologies and the transition to a sustainable and decent society with an economy that works over the long-term are difficult, complex, and intertwined problems with many possible answers.

In contrast to Lomborg, I believe that the public wants to hear good news and is hungry for authentic vision, committed leadership, and real solutions. There are some reasons for controlled optimism, but Lomborg and others like him offer denial disguised as optimism. They do so by restricting the context of the conversation and by conveying an impression of analytical precision where there is none, and where often none is possible. They avoid difficult political, moral, and value issues and presume to say more than can be legitimately said. The world is not as transparent to statistics as Lomborg thinks. But saying so would not have created much of a stir, certainly not in the right-wing press that seized on *The Skeptical Environmentalist* like "manna from heaven."

More importantly, aside from the cases in which Lomborg

airily dismisses contrary evidence, his optimism is held aloft by assumptions that markets will perform rationally and benign technologies will be adopted on schedule. But markets undisciplined by robust democratic politics do not act for the long-term good, nor do they automatically preserve nonpriced goods such as public health, economic fairness, resilient ecologies, climatic stability, endangered species, open spaces, culture, and our grandchildren's future. To the contrary, they mostly undermine democratic institutions and divert attention from the long-term and public goods. And, yes, some technologies have great promise, but their adoption in the limited time available to us will require political choices and public investment. The market, long rigged to fossil fuels and mass consumption will not do such things automatically as Lomborg presumes. Do we have the know-how and technology to make a transition to a better world? Probably. Do we have the foresight and political will to do so? Not yet. Do we have the time necessary to avoid global trauma? Who could possibly know? The answers can only be given over time by an engaged and informed citizenry and implemented by effective political institutions.

The buzz over *The Skeptical Environmentalist* has subsided. Lomborg himself has been censured by the Danish Research Agency for his biases and distortions of science. But a great deal of damage was done. To the casually informed, Lomborg's appearance of objectivity was misleading and confused large issues, offering a rationale for continuing business as usual. For those on the far right, he provided false legitimacy and further reason for procrastination. From this episode we should learn to study our critics carefully and respond quickly and forcefully. But most important, we should learn to balance the truth about the state of the world as best we can understand it with hope and a compelling vision of a world better than that in prospect.

Challenges

seven

Four Challenges of Sustainability

The destiny of the human species is to choose a truly great but brief, not a long and dull career.

–NICHOLAS GEORGESCU-ROEGEN, *THE ENTROPY LAW AND THE ECONOMIC PROCESS*

The concept of sustainability first came to public notice in Wes Jackson's work on agriculture in the late 1970s and Lester Brown's *Building a Sustainable Society* and Robert Allen's *How to Save the World* in 1980. The Brundtland Commission made sustainability a central feature of its 1987 report, defining it as meeting the needs of the present generation without compromising the ability of future generations to do the same.[1] Their definition confused sustainable growth, an oxymoron, and sustainable development, a possibility. Ambiguities notwithstanding, the concept of sustainability has become the keystone of the global dialogue about the human future. But what exactly do we intend to sustain and what will that require of us?

Such questions would have had little meaning to generations prior to, say, 1950, when nuclear annihilation became possible. Other than a collision between Earth and a large meteor there was no conceivable way that civilization everywhere could have been radically degraded or terminated. But now any well-informed high-school student could make a long list of ways in which humankind could cause its own demise, ranging from whimpers to bangs. The dialogue about sustainability is about a change in the human trajectory that will require us to rethink old assumptions and engage the large questions of the human condition that some presume to have been solved once and for all.

The things that cannot be sustained are clear. The ongoing militarization of the planet along with the greed and hatred that feeds it are not sustainable. Sooner or later a roll of the dice will come up Armageddon whether in the Indian subcontinent, in the Middle East, or by an accidental nuclear weapons launch or acts of a rogue state or terrorists. A world with a large number of desperately poor cannot be sustained, because they have the power to disrupt the lives of the comfortable in ways that we are only beginning to appreciate and that would not be worth sustaining anyway. The perpetual enlargement of the human estate cannot be sustained because it will eventually overwhelm the capacity and fecundity of natural systems and cycles. The unrestrained development of any and all technology cannot be sustained without courting risks and adverse consequences that we often see only when it is too late. A world of ever-increasing economic, financial, and technological complexity cannot be sustained because sooner or later it will overwhelm our capacity to manage. A world divided by narrow, exclusive, and intense allegiances to ideology or ethnicity cannot be sustained because its people will have too little humor, compassion, forgiveness, and wisdom to save themselves. Unrestrained automobility, hedonism, individualism, and conspicuous consumption cannot be sustained because they take more than they give back. A spiritually impoverished world cannot be sustained because meaninglessness, anomie, and despair will corrode the desire to be sustained and the belief that human-ity is worth sustaining. But these are the very things that dis-tinguish the modern age from its predecessors. Genuine sus-tainability, in other words, will come not from superficial changes but from a deeper process akin to humankind grow-ing up to a fuller stature.)

The question, then, is not whether we will change, but whether the transition will be done with more or less grace and whether the destination will be desirable or not. The barriers to a graceful transition to sustainability, whatever forms it may take, are not so much technological as they are social, political, and psychological. It is possible that we will be paralyzed by information overload leading to a kind of psychic numbness.[2] It is possible that we will suffer what Thomas Homer-Dixon calls an "ingenuity gap," in which problems outrun our problem-solving capacities.[3] It is possible that the sheer scale and com-plexity of human systems will become utterly unfathomable, hence unmanageable. It is possible that we will fail to compre-hend the nature of nature sufficiently to know how to live well on the Earth in large numbers. It is possible that we will fail to make a smooth transition because of political ineptitude and a lack of leadership and/or because power is co-opted by corpo-rations and private armies. It is possible that we will fail because powers of denial and wishful thinking cause us to underestimate the magnitude of our problems and to overlook better possibilities. And it is possible that we might fail because of what can only be called a condition of spiritual emptiness. The challenges of sustainability come hard on the heels of a century in which perhaps as many as 200 million people were killed in wars, ethnic conflicts, and extermination camps, taking a psychic toll that we dimly understand.

On the other hand it is possible, and I think likely, that the challenge of survival is precisely what will finally bring humankind together in the realization of the fragility of civi-lization and the triviality of most of our causes relative to this one central issue. The overall challenge of sustainability is to avoid crossing irreversible thresholds that damage the life systems of Earth while creating long-term economic, political, and moral arrangements that secure the well-being of present and future generations. We will have to acknowledge that the Enlightenment faith in human reason is, in some measure, wrong. But this does not mean less enlightenment, but rather a more enlightened enlightenment tempered by the recognition of human fallibility—a more rational kind of reason. In this light the great discovery of the modern era is not how to make nuclear fire, or alter our genes, or communicate at the speed of light but, rather, the discovery of our interconnectedness and implicatedness in the web of life. Our challenge is to comprehend what that awareness means in every area of life in order to calibrate human demands with what the Earth can sustain. Broadly speaking, the transition to sustainability poses four challenges.

First, we need more accurate models, metaphors, and measures to describe the human enterprise relative to the biosphere. We need a compass that defines true north for a civilization long on means and short on direction. On the one hand the conventional wisdom describes us as masters of the planet destined to become ever more numerous and rich without explaining how this is possible or why it might be desirable. In contrast, Howard and Elisabeth Odum argue "that many, if not all, of the systems of the planet have common properties, organize in similar ways, have similar oscillations over time, have similar patterns spatially, and operate within universal energy laws."[4] From the perspective of systems ecology, the efflorescence of humanity in the twentieth century is evidence of a natural pulsing. But having exhausted much of the material basis for expansion, like other systems, we are entering a down cycle, a "long process of reorganizing to form a lesser economy on renewable resources" before another upward pulse.[5] The pattern of growth/retreat found by the Odums in all systems stands in marked contrast to the rosy assumptions of perpetual economic growth. So, too, the prescriptions that follow. For the Odums smart policy would include plans for a prosperous descent, to avoid an otherwise catastrophic collapse. The specific tasks they propose are to "stabilize capitalism, protect the Earth's production of real wealth, and develop equity among nations."[6]

Archeologist Joseph Tainter proposes a similar model based on the rise and collapse of complex societies. Collapse eventually occurs when "investment in sociopolitical complexity . . . reaches a point of declining marginal returns."[7] In Tainter's view, this is "not a fall to some primordial chaos, but a return to the normal human condition of lower complexity."[8] Patterns of declining marginal returns, he believes, are now evident in some contemporary industrial societies in areas of agriculture, minerals and energy production, research, health care, education, and military and industrial management. Like the Odums, Tainter regards expansion and contraction as parts of a normal process. But how might we know whether we are in one phase or the other? The answer requires better accounting tools that relate human wealth generation to some larger measure of biophysical wealth. The Odums propose the concept of Emergy or what they define as "the available energy of one kind that has to be used up directly and indirectly to make a product or service."[9] By their accounting, the amount of embodied energy in solar equivalent units gives a more accurate picture of our relative wealth than purely financial measures. Others are developing different tools for the same purpose of including natural capital otherwise left out of purely economic accounting.

Second, the transition to sustainability will require a marked improvement and creativity in the arts of citizenship and governance.[10] There are some things that can be done only by an alert citizenry acting with responsive and democratically controlled governments. Only governments moved by an ethically robust and organized citizenry can act to ensure the fair distribution of wealth within and between generations. Only governments prodded by their citizens can act to limit risks posed by technology or clean up the mess afterward. Only governments and an environmentally literate public can choose to adopt and enforce standards that move us toward a cradle-to-cradle materials policy. Only governments acting on a public mandate can license corporations and control their activities for the public benefit over the long-term. Only governments can create the financial wherewithal to rebuild ecologically sound cities and dependable public transportation systems. Only governments acting with an informed public can set standards for the use of common property resources including the air, waters, wildlife, and soils. And only governments can implement strategies of resilience that enable the society to withstand unexpected disturbances. Resilience means dispersed, not concentrated, assets, control, and capacity. A resilient society, for instance, would have widely dispersed manufacturing, many small farms, many small cities and towns, greater self-reliance, and few if any technologies vulnerable to catastrophic failure, acts of God, or human malice. Sustainability, in short, constitutes a series of public choices that require effective institutions of governance and a well-informed democratically engaged citizenry.

The third challenge, then, is to inform the public's discretion through greatly improved education. The kind of education needed for the transition to sustainability, however, has little to do with improving SAT or GRE scores or advancing skills necessary to an expansionist phase of human culture. "During growth," write the Odums, "emphasis was on getting new information ... but as resource availability declines, emphasis [will be] on efficiency in teaching information that we already have."[11] They suggest a curriculum organized around the study of the relationships between energy, environment, and economics and how these apply across various scales of knowledge. Students of all ages will need the kind of education and skills appropriate to building a society with fewer cars but more bicycles and trains; fewer large power plants but more windmills and solar collectors; fewer super-markets and more farmers' markets; fewer large corporations and more small businesses; less time for leisure but more good work to do; and less public funding but more public spirit. From the Odums' perspective this is a generation that must foster the regeneration of natural capital of soils, forests, watersheds, and wild areas; clean up the toxic messes from the expansionist phase; restore sustainably habitable cities; relearn the practices of good farming; and learn the arts of powering civilization on efficiency and sunlight. Education appropriate to their future, not least, will require the courage to provide "intellectual leadership for the long-run" based on a clear understanding of where we stand relative to larger cycles and trends.[12]

It is easy, however, to offer long lists of solutions and still not solve the larger problem. The difficulty, once identified by E. F. Schumacher, is that human problems, like those posed by the transition to sustainability, are not solvable by rational means alone. These are what he called "divergent" problems, formed out of the tensions between competing perspectives that cannot be solved but can be transcended.[13] In contrast to "convergent" problems that can be solved by logic and method, divergent problems can only be resolved by higher forces of wisdom, love, compassion, understanding, and empathy. The logical mind does not much like divergent problems because it operates more easily with "either/or, or yes/no . . . like a computer."[14] Recognizing the challenge of sustainability as a series of divergent problems leads to the fourth and most difficult challenge of all.

The transition to sustainability will require learning how to recognize and resolve divergent problems, which is to say a higher level of spiritual awareness. By whatever name, some-thing akin to spiritual renewal is the sine qua non of the transition to sustainability. Scientists in a secular culture are often uneasy about matters of spirit, but science on its own can give no reason for sustaining humankind. It can, with equal rigor, create both the knowledge that will cause our demise or that necessary to live at peace with each other and nature. But the spiritual acumen necessary to solve divergent problems posed by the transition to sustainability cannot be just a return to some simplistic religious faith of an earlier time. It must be founded on a higher order of awareness that honors mystery, science, life, and death.

Specifically, the kind of spiritual renewal essential to sustainability must enable us to forgive the terrible wrongs at the heart of the bitter ethnic and national rivalries of past centuries and move on. There is no convergent logic or scientific solution that will enable us to transcend self-perpetuating hatreds and habitual violence. The only solution to this divergent problem is a profound sense of forgiveness and mercy that rises above the convergent logic of justice. The spiritual renewal necessary for the transition must provide convincing grounds by which humankind can justify the project of sustainability. We are, in Lynn Margulis's words, "upright mammalian weeds."[15] But is this all that we are or all that we can be? If so, we have little reason to be sustained beyond the sheer will to live. Perhaps this is enough, but I doubt it.

A robust spiritual sense may not mean that we are created in the image of God, but it must offer hope that we may grow into something more than a planetary plague. A robust spirituality must help us go deeper in order to resolve what Ernest Becker once described as the "terror of death" that "haunts the human animal like nothing else."[16] The effort, to deny the reality of our death, he believed, serves as "a mainspring of human activity" including much that we now see cannot be sustained.[17] "Modern man is drinking and drugging himself out of awareness," he wrote," or he spends his time shopping, which is the same thing. . . . Taking life seriously means that whatever man does on this planet has to be done in the lived truth of the terror of creation, of the grotesque, of the rumble of panic underneath everything."[18] In words written shortly before his own death, Becker concluded that "The urge to cosmic heroism, then, is sacred and mysterious and not to be neatly ordered and rationalized by science and secularism."[19] No culture has gone farther than our own to deny individual mortality, and in the denying is the killing of the planet. A spirituality that allows us to face our own mortality honestly, without denial or terror, contains the seeds of the daily heroism necessary to preserve life on Earth. Instead of terror, a deeper spirituality would lead us to a place of gratitude and celebration.

eight

Leverage

I once asked a class to explain the Gulf of Mexico dead zone (which is roughly the size of New Jersey), the fact that 22 percent of U.S. teenagers are reportedly overweight or obese, and the possible relationships between the two. After an hour, they had filled the blackboard with boxes and arrows that included federal farm subsidies, U.S. tax law, chemical dependency, feedlots and megafarms, the rise of the fast-food industry, declining farm communities, corporate centralization, advertising, a cheap food policy, research agendas at land-grant institutions, urban sprawl, the failure of political institutions, cheap fossil energy, and so forth. Most of the things described by those boxes, however, resulted from decisions that were once thought to be economically rational or at least within the legitimate self-interest of the parties involved. But collectively they are an unfolding continental-scale disaster affecting the health of people and land alike.

The same connect-the-dots kind of exercise could be done to explain urban decay and land sprawl, a defense policy that undermines true security, a de facto energy policy that promotes inefficiency, transportation gridlock, and the failure to provide universal health care. Our individual and collective failure to comprehend and act on the connectedness of things is pervasive, systemic, and threatens our health and long-term prosperity. It deserves urgent national attention, but is scarcely noticed. Why is this so?

First, we have organized our national affairs to create persistent gridlock reflecting the founders' fear of excessive government and true democracy. Authority is divided between local, state, and national governments and then between executive, judicial, and legislative branches. At the federal level, dozens of House and Senate committees and subcommittees oversee the nation's water, air, wildlife, lands, and resources.[1] Within the executive branch, environmental policy is a continual negotiation between various cabinet agencies and subagencies with competing agendas. As a result we have no national environmental policy for agriculture affecting 700 million acres, which is the largest source of water pollution. We have no comprehensive and farsighted national energy policy. Instead, in these and other areas we have a patchwork of laws and regulations inconsistently enforced at various levels of government, often working at cross-purposes, and in jeopardy from a hostile administration and court system. Almost without exception these laws and regulations operate after environmental damage has occurred, and most conflict with other statutes that aim to promote economic growth. Further, laws governing pollution tend to move pollutants from one medium to another. So, for example, we scrub SO_2 from power plants only to dispose toxic sludge on land. We "clean" water only to disperse toxic-laced solids on farmland or landfills. Pollution control becomes a kind of giant shell game by which we move pollutants between air, water, groundwater, and land.

Similarly, the hodgepodge of laws and regulations that govern chemical pollution are easily corrupted and constitute no effective protection to human or ecosystem health. Of some 75,000 chemicals in common use, only a few have been tested for a full range of health effects. Such tests do not include how one chemical interacts with others even though it is known that those interactions can sometimes increase toxicity by orders of magnitude. Nothing in the law and little in our political habits so far causes us to seek out better alternatives to the use of hazardous chemicals. So the debate tends to revolve around the rate at which we can legally poison each other.

It did not—and does not—have to be this way. In 1969 the National Environmental Policy Act (NEPA) described a different course intended to develop a systemic, unified, and long-term approach that would "use all practicable means and measures . . . to create and maintain conditions under which man and nature can exist in productive harmony." Although widely emulated in other countries, the promise of NEPA in the United States has not been realized.[2] The prospect of a systemic and farsighted approach to environmental policy was undermined from the beginning by the inherent limitations of fragmented government, by entrenched economic interests with easy access to the White House and members of Congress, by hostile courts, and by the tendency of industries to "capture" the agencies created to regulate them. Relative to the goals set forth in NEPA, the challenge of preserving biodiversity, and the ultimate challenge of building a society and world that can be sustained within the carrying capacity of the biosphere, U.S. environmental policy, despite many strengths, is a nickel solution for a dollar problem.

Its failure, moreover, is excused by our attitudes toward government generally. For twenty years or more we've stewed in the odd notion that "government is the problem" and some-times it is. But corporations, state governments, citizen apathy, and fanaticism of one kind or another can be problems as well. Extreme interpretations of individualism and property rights combined with a pervasive suspicion of government, for example, continually undermine the idea that public problems can and ought to be solved publicly, hence the possibility of doing so. Candidates, funded by interests wanting less public scrutiny, run for office on antigovernment platforms, pledging to do their best to limit governmental power while leaving that of corporations unimpeded. The United States has a long tradition of libertarian attitudes that serve to justify the ecological cacophony of sprawl, pollution, and waste. "What is missing from American environmental policy," says political scientist Richard Andrews, "is a coherent vision of common environmental good that is sufficiently compelling to generate sustained public support for government action to achieve it."[3]

There is a second reason for failure, which is inherent in the limitations of the reigning theories of economics. It is old news that, relative to our real wealth, the practice of mainstream economics and contemporary accounting methods conceal as much as they reveal. They do not, for example, account for the "services" of natural systems such as pollination, water purification, or recycling of organic matter.[4] Nor do they properly account for the loss of natural capital such as soils, forests, or species diversity.[5] The theory of economics, in either its classical or neoclassical version, followed industrialization and closely mirrored the reality thus created. It was a theory derived in full innocence of how the world works as a physical system and why this might be important, even for the economy. It could not account for what the economy did, because it could not take account of what it was undoing.

In no instance is this more evident than in the way we allocate investment by discounting future outcomes back to some purported net present value. A dollar in hand today, in other words, is worth more than a $1.10 a year from now. The practice is geared to maximize short-term benefits, often at a substantial long-term cost. Discounting the future means that we place little value on the possibilities of severe loss or even catastrophe a few decades hence. More shopping malls now trump concern for the decline in biodiversity; more highways now trump the need for farmland that could be needed by midcentury; more fossil energy now trumps concern about climatic change ahead. And so it goes, with the interests of our grandchildren discounted to zero. The practice of discounting, in economist Colin Price's words, "cannot be justified."[6] What can be justified is a "cold and rational altruism, driven by a belief in the propriety of sharing with later times the things we have valued, in the time which has been given to us."[7]

That much is well documented but widely ignored by defenders of doctrinal purity or acolytes of the myth of unfettered free markets. Beneath the formal theory there are crucial assumptions about what makes humans tick. Economic theory has it that we are, plain and simple, maximizers of our self-interest and that we know well enough what this is and how best to achieve it. But little in the human record supports such notions. We are, surely, far more complicated critters, as anyone who studies the effects of clever advertising or propaganda well knows. We are moved by many things beyond simple calculations of economic self-interest: fame, glory, power, group protection, nationalism, values, the prospect of salvation, sex, virtue, duty, and sometimes by plain orneriness, sometimes transcendence. The failure of economics to account for such things, too, is both widely remarked and ignored.

From such assumptions it is believed to be the height of rationality to ask, first, the cost of a thing, not whether it is a good thing to make or to do or how it fits with other priorities and values. The proper answer to "how much does it cost" is "relative to what and to whom and over what period of time?" Unable or unwilling to ask such questions, supposed cost is the most frequent reason given for not doing something otherwise good or necessary. In this intellectual and moral vacuum, we lose sight of the simple fact, as the late Donella Meadows put it, that "we don't get to choose which laws, those of the economy or those of the Earth, will ultimately prevail."[8] That being so, the result is that short-term wealth for a few is purchased at the cost of long-term prosperity for all.

There are certainly other reasons that we fail to perceive systemic causes and act accordingly, including overspecialization, reductionism, discipline-centric education, and the "dumbing down" of many things. But the point is that we've created a global system that may be an ecological absurdity but it is neither accidental nor incomprehensible. Rather, it is the result of decisions and choices we've made about how we conduct public affairs and how we evaluate our success. More to the point, are there places in the system where different decisions and relatively small reforms can produce large environmental results? Ecologist Norman Myers has identified one possibility: the $1.4 trillion in "perverse" subsidies worldwide that "exert adverse effects of both environmental and economic sorts over the long run" in fishing, agriculture, mining, road building, logging, and energy extraction and use.[9] Perverse subsidies are the sort Paul Hawken describes, by which "the government subsidizes energy costs so that farmers can deplete aquifers to grow alfalfa to feed cows that make milk that is stored in warehouses as surplus cheese that does not feed the hungry."[10] Eliminating such subsidies would go a long way to reducing overfishing, excessive road building, energy inefficiency, deforestation, and the loss of biodiversity.

In the United States specifically, estimates of subsidies for the automobile range from $400 billion to $730 billion. Levied as a tax on gasoline this amounts to something between $3.75 and $7.00 per gallon. Moreover, the Pentagon, prior to the war with Iraq, was spending about $50 billion alone to ensure U.S. access to Persian Gulf oil. The cost of that war adds billions more.[11] Traffic congestion in sixty-eight major cities costs another $78 billion in lost productivity, 6.8 billion gallons of wasted fuel, and 4.5 billion hours (and a fair amount of sanity) for drivers sitting in long lines of blue haze. Ending the large array of subsidies for automobiles over, say, ten years would help other modes of transportation become more viable and would enable us to rethink the design of urban areas to minimize the need for transport in the first place.

Economist Robert Frank has identified another leverage point: a tax on consumption aimed to eliminate the proliferation of luxury goods. "Our houses are bigger and our automobiles are faster . . . than ever before," he writes, but "we have less time for family and friends, and less time for sleep and exercise . . . our streets are dirty and congested. Our highways and bridges are in disrepair, placing countless lives in danger. And the misery in our inner cities continues unabated."[12] Although not primarily an environmental tax, a tax on luxury goods would save the resources that now fuel consumption. Frank's argument is roughly parallel to that given by economists to curb pollution by taxing it. At the same time he proposes to remove taxes from savings. Others propose more sweeping environmental taxes aimed at removing taxation from income and putting it on things we do not want, such as pollution and inefficiency. There are proposals for specific taxes called "feebates" that set energy performance standards above or below which buyers are given rebates or charged fees. Other countries, notably the Netherlands and New Zealand, have developed practical national "Green Plans," with targeted reductions in energy and resource use and lifecycle cost accounting.

The point is simply that there are good ways to improve our situation, reduce costs, increase fairness within and between the generations, eliminate a great deal of environmental damage, and create a sustainable prosperity while appealing to both liberals and conservatives. There are acceptable possibilities, in other words, to solve environmental problems in ways that promote the larger good without undue sacrifice now. What we lack is the mindset to see connections between things. In a real sense we do not have environmental problems we have perceptual problems, and what we've failed to see is the human enterprise and our little enterprises connected in space and time in more ways and at more levels than we could ever count. Once we've fully absorbed the reality of our interdependence in space and time, the rest is a great deal easier.

Is it possible to organize our public affairs and private lives in ways that honor the integrity of the whole over the long-term? No one I know thought more deeply or creatively about this question than Donella Meadows. Toward the end of a brilliant and vibrant life, she concluded that to change paradigms "you keep pointing at the anomalies and failures in the old paradigm, you come yourself, loudly, with assurance from the new one, you insert people with the new paradigm in places of public visibility and power. You don't waste time with reactionaries; rather you work with active change agents and with the vast middle ground of people who are open-minded." There are no "cheap tickets to system change," she wrote, "You have to work at it." And you have to "madly let go" of fear, greed, narrowness, and sometimes willful blindness to the connectedness of things.[13]

nine

A Literature of Redemption

re·deem to buy back; to liberate by payment; to free by force; to change for the better; to free from a lien; to remove the obligation; to make good; to atone for; to offset the bad effect of; to make worthwhile . . .

—MERRIAM WEBSTER'S SEVENTH NEW COLLEGIATE DICTIONARY

A century of world wars, gulags, torture, ethnic cleansing, saturation bombing, terrorism, mutual assured destruction, arms races, and random butchery has all but eliminated the optimism about human progress that existed a century ago. Even the end of the Cold War has not resulted in a new era of peace. Instead, conflicts multiply and ever more fearsome weapons proliferate. The word "progress" is now mostly applied to our gadgetry, not to moral improvement. Ahead? Who knows. God is dead, as Nietzsche would have it, but this belief has not resulted in any flowering of the human condition. In time, as Dostoyevsky noted, people so liberated would not be purged of false beliefs as much as they would come to believe anything. And so the age-old problem of human evil persists, now magnified by a level of technology unimaginable even a few years ago. The number of victims grows, anger multiplies, and violence and hatred feed on each other.[1]

There is no technology, no technique, no amount of cleverness that can break the cycles of hatred and violence in the Middle East, or Northern Ireland, or Rwanda, or the Balkans. Nor is there any technical solution to the kind of cold, unholy efficiency that created Auschwitz, Buchenwald, or the torture chambers of any number of present-day governments. These are, again, divergent problems that must be resolved by self-awareness, mercy, compassion, forgiveness, and justice, not logic. Whatever one's God, his/her apparent absence comes at a highly inconvenient moment, for never has humanity needed possibilities of transcendence more. Never have we had greater need for categories of thought that help us to resolve, rejoin, reconcile, bind together, render whole, and finally, to be redeemed. Such words sound archaic to the modern ear. They lack the sizzle of high technology and have none of the digital self-assurance of modern science. The concepts behind the words represent forgotten modes of thinking and being. And they require us to do things that are hard to do.

Resolution of divergent problems requires us, first, to think beyond self-interest and calculation, a difficult thing in any age, but particularly in one so enamored of the idea of individual rights. The resolution of divergent problems requires the moral and intellectual clarity to get the names of things right. Because we've mistaken security for weapons; identity for race, gender, or nationality; prosperity for affluence; power for domination; and freedom for license, ours is the most muddled age ever. Resolution of divergent problems further requires an extraordinary level of empathy with others beyond our own group and a depth of self-awareness that deflates the pretensions of inclusiveness. Hardest of all, it requires us to see our own culpability in tragedies easily blamed on others. Resolution of divergent problems, in short, requires a robust moral imagination that is able to see possibilities otherwise foreclosed by ignorance, hatred, and coldness.

Moral imagination, however, is the most difficult thing of all. There is no formula for the enlightenment of the human mind or for thawing the human heart, but there are ways that moral imagination can be developed. The end of slavery in 1865, for example, did not end racism in the United States. To the contrary the subsequent years were full of violence and discrimination. A new consciousness, however, began and continued to flower in the writings of Frederick Douglass, W. E. B. DuBois, Richard Wright, William Faulkner, Eudora Welty, Flannery O'Connor, Ralph Ellison, Lillian Smith, Ernest Gaines, and Alice Walker. A literature of redemption sprouted from the barren soil of slavery and is still growing. If there is hope for ending racism once and for all it is rooted in our capacity to comprehend what it meant to be a slave, to be despised for no other reason than color, to be invisible even in a society that deemed itself "free." That literature made it possible for those so treated to tell their stories and to say what needed to be said. White America needed to hear W. E. B. DuBois say that the white history of his day was propaganda written by men "who would compromise with truth."[2] It needed to hear Lillian Smith, a white woman writing in 1943, say,

> The burden our fathers had believed to be the "colored race," was our own historical past, the weight on our spirits was that of our childhood, the change we felt unable to make was a change in ourselves. We were beginning to see how entwined are the white man's beliefs about sin and sex and segregation and money, and his mother, and his wife, and himself; how they loop over each other and send out roots into the mythic mind, then climb into the rational mind, making a jungle hard to find a way through.[3]

A literature of redemption made it possible for others to *feel* what it was like to be a slave or to be abused because of color. And it made it possible to understand how bigotry germinates in the soil of ignorance, poverty, backwardness, demagoguery, and moral confusion. This literature did not instantly turn racists into people of reason, but it did provide a mirror to the larger society reflecting hypocrisy and injustice and thereby making it harder to be racist. It gave hope to those mistreated, and it established that a moral debt had to be paid in order to redeem the promise of a society in which all men were created equal. That literature gave voice and courage to the civil rights movement in the United States and all subsequent efforts to fulfill ancient promises of fairness, decency, and justice. But above all it established the fact of our common humanity living within a moral ecology, no part of which can be impaired without impairing the larger whole.

Conservationists are now engaged in a struggle to preserve biological diversity, an effort that implicitly questions human domination of nature and the extent of our moral responsibilities. Do we owe moral consideration to individual animals or to species or ecosystems? Does moral consideration apply only to those life forms that can reciprocate? Or those that suffer? Can we even know such things? Do obligations end with ecologically enlightened self-interest that counts all that we might lose in a biologically impoverished world? Or must we recognize rights intrinsic to other life forms, whatever their usefulness to us? If so, how far might such rights extend? Must our moral calculus include the likely interests of future generations? To ask such questions is to reveal problems far too complex to solve with anything like intellectual finality. It is easy, particularly for academics, to get caught up in interesting puzzles of this sort and miss the larger point altogether. The fact is that we stand on the edge of an abyss unbridgeable by science and intellect alone. Eventually we will have to *feel* the truth of the matter.

In various ways authors like DuBois, Smith, Faulkner, and Gaines helped us to feel the truth of human equality, expanding the awareness that all humans, regardless of circumstance, are entitled to equal protection under law. They had to challenge the idea that blacks were, as the Supreme Court put it in the Dred Scott decision, "beings of an inferior order [lacking] rights which the white man was bound to respect."[4] To do so these writers appealed to the foundational documents of America—the Bible, the Declaration of Independence, and the Constitution. But their larger appeal was to our common sense of decency and to our capacity for empathy.

No such foundation exists to resolve questions of environmental and interspecies ethics, and beyond the boundary of species, empathy is hard to arouse. The problem is not simply the differences between humans and other life forms, it is also an intellectual distancing traceable, in part, to Rene Descartes and his heirs who placed an emotional Iron Curtain around science itself. No good scientist could become emotionally connected to the object of research. In time, it came to be widely assumed, in Donald Griffin's words, "that human mental experiences are the only kind that can conceivably exist."[5] A decade later Griffin wrote,

> Much of twentieth-century science has gradually slipped into an attitude that belittles nonhuman animals. Subtle but effective nonverbal signals to this effect emanate from much of the scientific literature. Physical and chemical science is assumed to be more fundamental, more rigorous, and more significant than zoology. Modern biology revels in being largely molecular, and this inevitably diverts attention away from the investigation of animals for their own sakes.[6]

In contrast to Cartesian assumptions that animals are unthinking, unfeeling, and machinelike, evidence is mounting that something like mind pervades much, if not all, of the animal kingdom. According to Griffin, it is likely "that mental experiences . . . are widespread, at least among multicellular animals, but differ greatly in nature and complexity."[7] That conclusion and more is born out in the research of Jane

Goodall, Bernd Heinrich, and Roger Fouts, among others, who have documented complex animal behaviors including problem solving, use of tools, memory, and emotional lives that resemble our own. "Our current systems of law and morality," says Fouts, "is based on an imagined gap between humans and nonhumans" where none exists.[8] The logical conclusion drawn a long time ago by none other than Charles Darwin is that our moral progress will not be complete until we extend our compassion to all people and to all species.[9] And more than compassion. As legal scholar Steven Wise puts it, "It should now be obvious that the ancient Great Wall that has for so long divided humans from every other animal is biased, irrational, unfair, and unjust. It is time to knock it down."[10]

Like the human history of discrimination, domination, and oppression, our behavior toward animals has been wrong, but concealed by the comfortable verities of power, ignorance, and hard heartedness. We have been taught to respect life while we negate it in hundreds of daily acts. Such acts have caused an untold amount of suffering throughout the rest of the animal kingdom that must now be made right by the one calling itself *Homo sapiens*. The fact is that the qualities we've deemed to be solely human represent one part of a spectrum that defies easy demarcation from one level to another, and humankind is only a small part of a much larger enterprise. Science, too, is a small part of a larger moral ecology aiming to redeem better possibilities than those in prospect.

ten

Diversity

By all credible accounts the diversity of species is in sharp decline, headed toward what Richard Leakey and Roger Lewin call "the sixth extinction."[1] The causes of species decline include population growth, economic expansion, pollution, climate change, mining, logging, urban sprawl, overfishing, and the displacement of indigenous peoples. The legal and administrative protections placed between endangered species and eternity work, at best, in a limited fashion for a time. Our successes in preservation, as David Brower once noted, are temporary while our failures are permanent. But the problem is not limited to the decline of biological diversity. Many of the same forces that erode biological diversity jeopardize diversity of all kinds, including that of languages and culture. The modern world, it seems, is at war with difference even while professing devotion to it.

The loss of diversity cannot be attributed, on the whole, to ignorance. Considerable effort has been and is being made to document the decline, but how much such information reaches the public or particular decision makers is hard to say. What is apparent, for those who wish to see, is an increasingly detailed and discouraging picture. E. O. Wilson believes that we could lose a quarter of the world's biodiversity over the next century, or with foresight and a bit of luck we might hold the loss to 10 percent.[2] Nor are we ignorant, for the most part, of the many reasons why diversity should be preserved. Self-interest, cultural prudence, and arguments in defense of the intrinsic rights of species converge on the same goal of saving all that can be saved. We know that it would be foolish to wantonly eliminate the many services provided by species and healthy ecosystems. Beyond arguments grounded in utility, however, we have powerful moral reasons to preserve species that provide no useful service to *Homo sapiens*. But neither argument has changed much relative to what needs to be changed if biological and cultural diversity is to be preserved; so species, languages, and indigenous cultures continue to spiral downward. One suspects that the effort to preserve diversity runs against deeper currents. We profess great devotion to that which we seem incapable of protecting, in large part, I think, because the very logic of modern culture aims everywhere for uniformity and control.

Modernization from its earliest beginnings formed around ideas such as progress, economic growth, and human superiority over nature and the goals of standardization, legibility, efficiency, and control. Lewis Mumford begins his magisterial history of technology, for example, with a discussion of the clock, which he describes as "the foremost machine of modern technics."[3] The widespread adoption of the clock in the fourteenth century led to the quantification of time and "a new medium of existence" in which "one ate, not upon feeling hungry, but when prompted by the clock: one slept, not when one was tired, but when the clock sanctioned it."[4] The irregularities of actual days and seasons, as well as those inherent in the human organism, were swept aside in favor of time that could be measured, counted, and made to count. The clock was followed in rapid succession by geometrically precise maps, double-entry bookkeeping, the art of perspective in painting, and the marriage of vision and quantification that, in Alfred Crosby's words, "snap the padlock—reality is fettered."[5] Ability to quantify visual space enabled Europeans to extend control in hitherto unimaginable ways and envision things yet to be invented, giving rise to still greater control and uniformity.

The same trend toward greater control became evident in European philosophy, science, and politics in the turbulent seventeenth century. "From 1630 on," notes philosopher Stephen Toulmin, "the focus of philosophical inquiries has ignored the particular, concrete, timely and local details of everyday human affairs: instead, it shifted to a higher, stratospheric plane, on which nature and ethics conform to abstract, timeless, general, and universal theories."[6] The dream of reason aimed to establish rational methods, an exact language, and a unified science, in other words, "a single project designed to purify the operations of the Human Reason by desituating them: that is, divorcing them from the compromising association of their cultural contexts."[7] This was nothing less than the triumph, temporary perhaps, of rationality over reasonableness, calculation over emotion, generality over particularity. The result, in Toulmin's words, was "injury to our commonsense ways of thought [and] confusion about some highly important questions."[8]

The search for certainty extended past the abstractions of philosophy and science to change how people related to physical reality as well. Early and inaccurate means of surveying land, for example, surrendered to precise land measurement based on Edmund Gunter's twenty-two-yard-long surveying chain.[9] This precise measurement permitted a market by which land became yet another commodity. According to the land ordinance of 1785, "surveyors shall proceed to divide the said territory into townships of 6 miles square, by lines running due north and south, and others crossing these at right angles."[10] The subsequent grid pattern marched westward from the Appalachian Mountains across prairies to the Pacific regardless of variations of topography, ecology, or the long-established use patterns of the natives who did not believe in owning land, or in right angles for that matter. In the twentieth century, the drive for standardization was applied to the workplace (Taylorism), to public economics as cost-benefit analysis, and to business operations, education, agriculture, forestry, urban planning, and governance. The culmination was what James C. Scott calls "a high modernist ideology . . . a muscle-bound version of the self-confidence about scientific and technical progress, the expansion of production, the growing satisfaction of human needs, the mastery of nature (including human nature), and above all, the rational design of social order commensurate with the scientific understanding of natural laws."[11]

The juggernaut of standardization, uniformity, and legibility is a product of large forces, including technological dynamism, the triumph of quantification, the need of the modern state to extend its control over its land and citizens, and that of capitalism to grow without limit. Whatever their differences, all converged around the goals of precise measurement, increasingly pervasive control, and growth of the human estate. The inevitable result was to increase scale, complexity, velocity, profitability, pollution, lethality, and bureaucracy and generate hidden costs and surprises. But the choices leading in this direction were not at all inevitable or even probable at the time they were made. The important point is that this particular form of modernization represents choices, and sometimes there were better choices to have been made and some that might still be made.

The well-advertised gains of modernization over the past two centuries are obvious, including greater material comfort, longer lives, increased mobility, and a huge gain in material wealth. On the other hand, any honest reckoning of the price we have paid and continue to pay for standardization must include the unaccounted costs such as the destruction of natural systems, social regimentation, militarization, the extermination of indigenous peoples, inequality, and more. Still other costs are hidden. In the words of one observer, part of the cost (of quantification) is that "inevitably meanings are lost . . . because it imposes order on hazy thinking, but this depends on the license it provides to ignore or reconfigure much of what is difficult or obscure."[12] And much is difficult and obscure, including the value of diversity itself in all of its manifestations and even the capacity to think diversely. It is logical that the drive for standardization and uniformity might someday impose a grid-like pattern to the ecology of our minds until we are permitted to have no thoughts without right angles.

On the other hand, the world is full of surprise and paradox and mocks the human pretension to mastery. As management, standardization, and uniformity have increased without limit, so have the number of unanticipated effects of all kinds. Often called "side effects," they are more accurately said to be logical outcomes that we weren't smart enough to foresee. Predictably, our attempts to render nature more orderly often backfire. Large dams, pesticides, wonder drugs, improved forests, highways, industrial agriculture and factory farms run afoul of larger forces and limitations. But the same applies everywhere, relentlessly. Human perversity or creativity, sometimes only a difference of perspective, will find ways to subvert clocks, walls, bureaucracy, straight lines, barriers, and regimentation. There are, in other words, limits to what we can control at any scale over any length of time, and there are larger forces that care not one iota for either capitalism, reasons of state, or big science and will, in due time, sweep all off the stage. Those limits, ecological, economic, political, organizational, and human were evident in the collapse of the Soviet Union. But it is no less likely that a capitalist society organized around a diminishing number of ever-larger corporations will also self-destruct. The belief that we might organize the entire planet for the convenience of capital and capitalists one-day will be seen as a kind of perverse and self-defeating foolishness. By the same token, the belief that we can render ourselves safe by building higher and thicker walls, imposing tighter surveillance, or developing ever more heroic and implausible technology will one day be seen as about as effective as a child hiding under bed covers in a thunder storm.

We struggle in vain to define either how the world is or how it works, in part because our language, minds, categories of thought, perceptions, values, and intellectual tools have been honed to control. But it is apparent that the logic of human control and mastery runs counter to the 3.8 billion years of evolution and that discrepancy is not a small flaw, but more like a fault line. The record of evolution is one of surprise, flow, networks of causes, unpredictability, nonlinearity, collapse, and creativity—all words describing what we see dimly and often wrongly. The very fact of biological diversity suggests humility about what we attempt to control and how we do it. The truth is that diversity of any kind could not have occurred in a thoroughly managed world and it cannot be protected in a world that some purport to manage thoroughly for whatever good cause. The logic of the modern economy and state runs counter to the flow of evolution, and something will have to give. Given the odds, it would be foolish to wager on the alacrity, wisdom, and wherewithal of economists, businessmen, media pundits, or politicians.

Our situation is captured in Einstein's famous observation that the same kind of thinking that created a problem cannot fix it. The preservation of diversity will require a different manner of thinking that runs counter to much of conventional wisdom, including that described as environmental. In other words, the cause of protecting diversity must be broadened, deepened, and joined to other causes. If the destination is shrouded, at least the starting points are clear.

First, we should be clear about why diversity is important, and the strongest arguments are not first and foremost economic. To arguments of self-interest, prudence, and intrinsic rights—all true enough—we should add the idea of celebration of beauty that is inherent in the diversity of life and human culture. Arguments from self-interest or duty often sound like a Puritanical sermon running on too long, the point of which is that guilt will move us to better behavior. Sometimes it does, but it is more likely that we will be moved farther and to better ends by shorter sermons and the power of wonder, joy, and celebration. This is no more than to acknowledge Pascal's observation that "the heart has its reasons which reason knows nothing of."

Second, the protection of diversity requires that we address the issue of economics, but on terms that the seventh generation out would find agreeable. "The juggernaut of technology-based capitalism will not be stopped," says E. O. Wilson, "but its direction can be changed."[13] Changing the direction of capitalism means rigorously applying the laws of capitalism to protect the natural capital of wildlife, ecosystems, soils, forests—all of those factors on which capitalism depends. It requires eliminating what Norman Myers calls "perverse subsidies" for excess and unprofitable logging, fishing, road building, and power plants. Further, redirection of the juggernaut will require limits on "the scale of human activities."[14] A logical, if problematic, beginning point would be something like a global version of the Sherman Antitrust Act of 1890 (rigorously enforced) to limit the size of corporations and make them accountable to the larger world interest. Nowhere is it written that we are to be ruled by distant and unaccountable economic powers or unresponsive governments. While we are at it we might toss out the habit of giving obeisance to pecuniary interests with the same disdain by which we once discarded the notion that Kings ruled by divine right.

Third, if we are to choose to protect diversity we will need leaders who frame the real issues of our time and help craft the public laws, instruments, and means by which we might do so. We need policies that enable the world to make a timely transition from fossil to renewable energy and others that stop the destruction of habitat. There are also larger questions having to do with the scale of the economy and the point at which further growth becomes, not just superfluous, but destructive. Soon, we will have to redress the growing income disparity between the rich and the poor and what could be an even larger gap between present and future generations. It is commonly assumed that the triumph of capitalism in the 1990s settled questions of the distribution of wealth once and for all in favor of the rich. But inequities worldwide continue to worsen; consequently, so do the incentives and capacity in much of the world to conserve biodiversity. In every way these are political issues and can only be resolved politically.

Fourth, for two centuries the Western world organized around the master idea of freedom. It was, and remains, a powerful idea that helped humanity surmount arbitrary authority of church, monarchy, and custom. But to traverse the topography of the century ahead we will need a larger master idea. As candidates, the concepts of diversity and sustainability have the drawback that they limit freedom, as presently understood. Most people will not accept such limits without understanding that freedom was never intended as license, rather it was known to entail personal restraint and the exercise of duties to the larger community.[15] There can be no freedom amidst social chaos, nor can there be freedom in a state of ecological ruin. This level of sophistication requires that people understand the linkages between human behavior and ecological health, which is to say a comprehension of how the world works as a system.

Finally, the protection of diversity will require a larger and yet more limited view of science and what it means to know. It is assumed, wrongly I think, that knowing is equivalent to measuring, explaining, and controlling. The protection of diversity will require, to the contrary, that we recognize reality and value that exist beyond our limited ability to measure and control. The fact is that diversity can be measured and described at a superficial level but can never be explained or known. The scientific impulse is to add something like "not yet," in the faith that we will, given time, figure it all out. I think it more likely that the right word is "never," in the recognition of the limits of human knowledge and the many ways that knowledge can be corrupted, co-opted, and misused. This is the kind of mature knowledge once proposed by Aldo Leopold and Rachel Carson, rooted in the recognition of the kinship of all life and the limits of human knowledge. It is a science driven by wonder and disciplined by humility, in the recognition that there are mysteries that we are powerless to name.

Reconstruction

eleven

The Uses of Prophecy

For three decades and more, Wendell Berry has written about farming, soil, nature, and community without ever becoming repetitious or boring. He is an agrarian, or more accurately, the preeminent agrarian. From Hesiod to the present no one has represented the agrarian cause with greater eloquence, logic, or consistency. The power behind his writing, however, is the close calibration between his words and the life he's lived—"a principled literary life," as Wallace Stegner once put it. If there are discerning readers two centuries hence, I have no doubt that Wendell Berry's novels, essays, and poetry will still be read. But there is cause to doubt whether Berry's agrarian philosophy will be more than a footnote in a history of technological expansion, urbanization, and economic growth until things come permanently undone. He is widely admired for his literary gifts and wisdom, yet much dismissed. Why is this so? What does it say about who we are and about our larger prospects? And what might be done about it?

Interpretations

The most common reaction to Wendell Berry is to concede his literary talents while dismissing the substance of what he has to say as nostalgia for a bygone but better time. Many can recall a time of prosperous farms and rural communities, places that fostered good children, decent citizens, competent people, land stewardship, and real patriots. The tens of thousands of visitors to Amish country in Ohio and Pennsylvania are daily testimony to the appeal of a life rooted in the land and in stable rural communities. For many, this is not nostalgia, but an awareness that in some places and at some times people did get the relation between culture and land right, and that remembrance haunts the modern mind. Jaquetta Hawkes, for example, once described rural England of the eighteenth century as characterized by a "creative, patient, and increasingly skilful love-making that persuaded the land to flourish."[1] Such times and places were not perfect by any means, but they did represent an exceptional quality of life. That such places are now mostly confined to memory is a fact to be lamented, but not undone because of changes in farming, culture, and society. More importantly, so goes the argument, the small farms favored by Berry would be inadequate to feed a growing world population. The necessity imposed by sheer numbers requires the industrialization of farming, which means large amounts of capital, large-scale farms, chemicals, food processing, and companies like ADM and ConAgra to feed the world. Others like James Lovelock arrive at roughly the same conclusion by a different route. Agriculture, they say, must be replaced by a technology-intensive food system in order to free land for wilderness, store carbon out of the atmosphere, preserve biological diversity, and stabilize the Earth's vital signs.

Second, most would say that the benign world described by the agrarians never truly existed. Farming and rural life were boring, hard, insecure, and sexist. The agrarian world, furthermore, was rooted in injustice because the land, here and elsewhere, was stolen from natives. Farm life was difficult and economically insecure. The agrarian world was dominated by men to the great disadvantage of women, children, and nature. The demands of farm work drove out the development of other talents and interests so that human potentials and real culture withered on the vine. Rural communities were often closed and hostile to social, religious, and cultural diversity. Agrarian communities, closed to outsiders, were "provincial" in outlook. At their worst, they were the violent, evil, and confining places described by William Faulkner. Agrarianism? Good riddance!

Agrarians must acknowledge that this indictment has some truth, but it is not the entire story. Farming has always meant hard work and economic insecurity that was compounded by exploitation by the crown, the nobility, and the church. In our own history, agrarianism flourished in New England for a time and in parts of the Midwest, but is now most evident in Amish communities. Its decline can be attributed to many things, including the fact that many farmers, as Berry says, did not come to stay but to make money, cashing out at the first opportunity. For the majority, however, the relentless pressure of the market undermined care for the land, cooperation, thrift, community, and permanence. In other words, most of what we know about farming and farm life is how it was done and lived out in situations where farmers and land alike were greatly exploited.

A third reaction to the agrarianism of Wendell Berry is to say that it is just not in our nature to scratch the soil, sow, reap, and live in settled communities. Agriculture is a ten-thousand-year-long aberration caused by overpopulation and the necessity to feed urban masses, a wrong turn in human evolution. Paul Shepard, for one, has argued that humans are really hunter-gatherers and that tending the soil was a late and unfortunate overlay on our true nature. A better society, he said, would be oriented to a kind of high technology hunting and gathering. But how are we to reenact the hunting-gathering ideal in a world organized along very different lines for the past ten thousand years? The only plausible answer is that we cannot.

A fourth view says that agrarianism, whether good, bad, or otherwise, was simply a stage in human evolution that has passed because our technological prowess is taking us in other, and presumably better directions. Food might soon be grown without anything like present-day farms and farmers or even soil. It is possible to create foodlike substances from oil in factories that require much technology and few people. Taking this a step further, professor Hans Moravic proposes that we even shed the body and "download" our minds into computers attached to machines that function like bodies with arms and legs. Since machines can be repaired, we would attain immortality of sorts. But assuming this is possible, what exactly would "we" be? Surely we would not be human in a way recognizable to us now. Our human nature is the result of a long conversation between the body, mind, spirit, culture, and physical nature. Mind is not separable from the body as Descartes and Moravic would have it. Nor is the "embodied mind" separable from the nature of places. Improvers such as Moravic intend an end run around mortality and with it our dependence on soil, rain, and the skill of the farmer. Food is replaced by the need for electricity. At mealtime one would plug in, not dine. More conveniently, perhaps our "progeny" could be engineered to photosynthesize directly with minds engineered to believe this to be an improvement. Whether Moravic's world could be made to "work" I do not know, but I do know that it represents a point of no return.

A fifth reaction to Wendell Berry is to say that in the best of all possible worlds we would live in predominantly agrarian communities as Berry proposes, but we aren't up to it. As Dostoyevsky's Grand Inquisitor in *Brothers Karamazov* puts it to a silent Christ, humanity is "weak, vicious, worthless, and rebellious . . . in the end they will lay their freedom at our feet, and say to us, 'make us your slaves, but feed us.'" Christ, in Dostoyevsky's telling, remains ambiguously silent. However said, this is the view of all those who purport to be a "supermarket to the world" or to "do it all for you" without any effort, skill, or even awareness on our part. There is no crime but hunger, as Dostoyevsky says, so whatever it takes to feed the world is permissible. Given the chance, we would trade the toil and insecurity of agriculture for the promise of ease, abundance, and security. And once the trade is consummated, we become accustomed to conveniences, luxury, and, as Wallace Stegner once said, all of those "things that once possessed could not be done without." Farming, in other words, is a burden that most farmers discard as soon as they are able. That view is rendered plausible by the history of farm technology from the middle of the nineteenth century to the present. With the notable exception of the Amish, farmers adopted virtually every device that promised higher production with less physical effort. In the process, farming as a way of life gave way to agribusiness. In short, there are good circumstances that we cannot sustain and visions that we cannot live up to.

Victor Davis Hanson believes this to be the doomed fate of small-scale agriculture and small farmers:

> The sad history of complex societies, ancient and modern, argues that bureaucracies grow, never shrink, and so suggest that these futurists—not agrarian romantics—have seen the real forecast over the horizon. Unproductive citizens multiply, rarely wane. Taxation, urbanization, and specialization are the harvests of elite legitimizing and nuancing classes—government, insurance, advertising, law, finance—who feed and clone from ritual, regulation, and regimentation.[2]

The agrarian world is being crushed by the remorseless development of civilization and by the lack of courage to return to "a common culture of peers, life away from the vortex of pelf and publicity, a firmness with the poor as well as the wealthy, an embrace of rural shame, a rejection of convenient urban guilt."[3] Hanson offers no hope for the family farm: "We are now in the third stage of a future that has no future, an agrarian Armageddon at the millennium where the family farm itself . . . will be obliterated."[4]

In some places, however, stable agrarian communities existed for many centuries. When they eventually declined or disappeared, it was not because rural people were weak, lazy, or incompetent. To the contrary, they mostly failed because of larger economic and political forces. Historically, European peasants were bled white by taxation. The English peasantry were forced to the margin by the enclosure of common lands and the political power, first of the landed nobility, and then by that of industrialists. The prosperous Russian peasants (kulaks) were coerced into collective farms by Stalin. In our own history, the decline of farms and farm communities is a complicated story of taxes, land prices, government policies, and the treadmill of technological improvement. As a result, throughout the twentieth century many left farming more from necessity than by choice. The deck was stacked against the farmer and particularly the small farmer. And that is not all.

Whatever status farmers once had has withered in the onslaught of the advertising, entertainment, and communication industries. Agrarian virtues of honesty, thrift, practical competence, and neighborliness have no place in the glittering, fast-paced, consumer-oriented world of Madison Avenue and Hollywood. A way of life dependent on soil, hard work, ecological competence, and devotion to place became a source of shame. Children of farmers could not help but compare their parents with the slick images of the smart city people living effortless, exciting lives as portrayed in magazines, catalogs, and the movies. But this is not the kind of individual weakness described by Dostoyevsky as much as it is evidence that we are vulnerable to the considerable applied powers of modern psychology and communications technology deployed to make us dependable customers. Advertising and entertainment industries have become adept at selling a life "style" requiring lots of cash and an agreeable willingness to part with it on a whim—further evidence of the corruption of society organized around the logic of finance capital and exploitation.

Finally, Page Smith had it right, I believe, when he described Wendell Berry as "*the* prophetic American voice of our day." This perspective may help to explain why he is both widely admired and often ignored. We don't much like prophets because they make us feel uneasy. They see things most prefer not to see and say things many wish went unsaid. They are ambiguous figures who point out the gap between an unhappy reality and better possibilities that reveals us for what we are. Instead of being forgiving and therapeutic, prophets are, as Abraham Heschel once wrote, "impatient of excuse, contemptuous of pretense and self pity."[5]

But prophets do not just condemn. They intend to move us toward better possibilities. They call to mind a time when we were better people, but they also look forward to a time when we might be restored to some semblance of grace, which is to say that they are accusatory and forgiving. Prophets are poised between the past and a better future. To dismiss Berry as simply nostalgic misses the point. He ought to be read as much as a futurist describing better possibilities as someone looking back to what once had been. To argue that his view of the past is mistaken is, I think, to misread both Berry and the historical record. Decent agrarian communities have existed and their various imperfections do not diminish that fact. Good small farms are known to be as productive as any agribusiness or more so, but without the ecological and social costs. And to dismiss agrarian possibilities that Berry describes on the grounds of necessity is to surrender our ability to choose to an unwarranted and unworthy technological, demographic, or economic determinism. To propose that we further technologize the food system or shed the body for some machinelike existence is sheer madness. But whether we are up to the challenge of going forward to an authentic agrarian future is another matter entirely.

The Powers of Denial

The obstacles to agrarianism of any sort are many, beginning with the obvious fact that we have built a massive infrastructure of pipelines, power plants, roads, bridges, airports, railroads, mines, factories, shopping malls, and so forth around the idea of permanent economic expansion powered by cheap fossil fuels. Much of that infrastructure is dangerous, vulnerable to terrorists, polluting, and obsolete. A sizeable portion of it is in need of repair and must soon be replaced. More important, industrialization is also embedded in our minds and limits our ability to imagine better possibilities. Industrialization rested on the simple and seductively powerful idea that we could exploit soils, forests, biological diversity, and minerals without adverse consequences and that doing so was akin to our rightful destiny. That idea is widely known to be wrong, even perversely so, but it still exerts a powerful hold on the public mind and public policies. Some find it difficult to consider the possibility that paying the full social and environmental costs would have radically changed the scale and scope of industrialization.

Agrarians, however, have always understood this. They give priority to honest accounting that includes soil, land, community, good work, and to agriculture as the foundation for culture. They believe, in Liberty Hyde Bailey's words, "that the farm and the backspaces have been the mother of the race" because "they beget men and women to be serious and steady and to know the value of every hour and of every coin that they earn; and whenever they are properly trained, these folk recognize the holiness of the earth."[6]

If that sounds quaint to some, the advantages of a new

kind of agrarianism in the twenty-first century—considering the alternatives—are increasingly compelling to others. Concern to preserve farms and farmland is evident in recent citizen initiatives across the country. The market for organic food is rising by double digits each year. Gardening programs exist in virtually every major city and in many schools. The sustainable agriculture movement, if not yet a major political force, has grown steadily for three decades. And after the events of 9/11 there is a powerful case to be made for a new agrarianism to secure the nation's food supply. The resilience that once characterized a distributed network of millions of small farms serving local and regional markets made it invulnerable to almost any conceivable external threat, to say nothing of the other human and social benefits that come from communities organized around prosperous farms.

That the political, economic, intellectual, and ecclesiastical leadership of the country largely ignores such things, says nothing about the wisdom of a new agrarianism and everything about the concentration of political, economic, and intellectual power and the hold that industrialism still has on the public mind. What passes for farm policy, for instance, is little more than a vast system of subsidies that enriches agribusiness and corporations while promoting overproduction and driving small farmers out of business here and elsewhere—all justified in the name of economic rationality. The deck is stacked higher than ever against agrarians. Why?

The answer is not simply that we have built a massive industrial infrastructure and therefore have no other options, rather, it is that we continually fail to implement better possibilities. But what stops us from making an effective and rapid transition from fossil fuels to efficiency and renewable energy? What stops us from pricing resources at their true costs? What prevents us from conserving farms and open spaces? By what logic do we fail to account for the costs of climate change or pollution? Why do we subsidize overcutting in the national forests or give minerals on public lands to large corporations for a pittance? Why do the already wealthy grow ever richer and the poor ever poorer? None of this is inevitable, but is a kind of willing sleepwalk toward the edge of an abyss. The industrial world, in other words, is not just a physical reality, it is a system of denial.

A large part of that system has to do with the corruption of our democracy by the largely unchecked power of corporations and the hugely wealthy. America is fast becoming a colony controlled by a small class of exploiters who have no allegiance to the land or democracy, and no sense of responsibility beyond that to maximize short-term shareholder value. They consider themselves to be a part of a global economy and no part of any particular place or local economy. Power, accordingly, has gravitated from citizens to corporations who do not consider themselves citizens at all and whose lobbyists diligently troll the halls of Congress and state legislatures to purchase votes, access, and absolution. Recent revelations about corporate accounting scandals are just that: recent revelations, the small tip of a very big iceberg. The pattern of abuse, which has been there all along, is once again exposed for what it is and has always been: a system seldom beholden to good public purpose and consistently aimed at further enriching the wealthy. And the public, once again, are given solemn promises of reform by public officials who are themselves indentured to the money class. A compliant media, a fully owned subsidiary, duly report such things between their advertisements. None of this is news to readers of Wendell Berry or to the merely alert.

We know that denial and political corruption requires the prior corruption of language. By some strange alchemy, the word "conservative" has been co-opted by those intending to conserve nothing except the rules of the game by which they are greatly enriched. That they wish to bamboozle should astonish no one; that they get away with it, however, depends on a high level of public drowsiness and gullibility. But that is an altogether more complicated thing—a kind of coconspiracy involving a combination of ignorance and apathy on one side and a desire to mislead on the other, all disguised by a language unhinged from reality. We come to believe that "Coca-Cola is the real thing" and by a similar logic that G. W. is a real president like, say, Lincoln, Roosevelt, or even Hoover for that matter. Perhaps we assume that none of this matters very much anyway because images are what count, not place, tradition, obligations, physical reality, or our long-term prospects. We are complicit in the corruption of language and in the very process whereby we are being dumbed down. Language, as George Orwell reminds us, "becomes ugly and inaccurate because our thoughts are foolish, but the slovenliness of our language makes it easier for us to have foolish thoughts."[7] And foolish thoughts we have in surplus, goaded on by television and the $300 billion spent by the advertising industry to promote foolishness.

One might expect that sloppy language would stand revealed as nonsense by the rigorous power of numbers. Alas, numbers in the service of denial are corrupt as well. One need look no further than the fictions offered up by economists that exclude biology, ecology, morality, and thermodynamics. The practice of capitalist bookkeeping has no debit column in which we would subtract the loss of soil, forests, water quality, wildlife, and countryside. What counts, as they say, is what can be easily counted. The "services of nature" such as water and air purification, decomposition of waste, pollination, soil fertility, and climate regulation—more elusive but no less real—are neglected, but that does not thereby make us wealthier. At best that neglect deceives and at worst it conceals the transfer of wealth from country to city and from future generations to the present, which is to say it is theft.

Denial does not end with politics, advertising, or economics, it has invaded the world of research and education. In *The Unsettling of America,* Berry describes the perversion of the intentions behind the creation of land-grant universities by which these institutions have become adjuncts to agribusiness. The problem has grown worse in the decades since the book's publication. Science, as Berry argues in *Life Is a Miracle*, has become increasingly absolute in its reach and in its pretensions of omniscience. New developments in genetic engineering, nanotechnology, and artificial intelligence threaten to take us beyond a point of no return, yet we seem to be unable to act with foresight. Intelligence, often confused with the encumbrance of learned degrees, is conspicuous by its absence in debates about science and the proper boundaries of technology, and this, too, has to do with an older corruption of language and words such as "progress" and "development." Educational and research institutions were fashioned as industries that over time became useful and beholden to other industries in the belief that they thereby served human progress and development, without much thought about what those words meant. In time, I think these words came to mean something far removed from what was once intended: an escape from the human condition itself.

This leads me to a final observation. Agrarian life places people in close contact with the cycles of birth and death. On the farm, something is always being born and growing or being led to slaughter and dying. Death is simply part of a natural cycle that farm children experience early on. That proximity to death as an everyday occurrence doesn't make it necessarily easier, but such circumstances may make death easier to comprehend and accept as part of the natural order of things. The closeness to birth, growth, decay, and death in the nurturing context of a farm have the effect of demystifying mortality and laying the psychological foundation for the healthy acceptance of our own death. The demise of small, diversified farms and the numbers of people in contact with farming, then, is not just a change in the way we produce food and organize the countryside, but a change in how we think about the basic facts of living and dying. Industrial agriculture conceals death on a massive scale, making it "efficient" and thereby ugly and sacrilegious.

Presently, we are witness to death on the largest scale imaginable. No day passes without news of the decline of species, seas, lands, forests, lakes, rivers, all spiraling downward into the destabilization of the planet's biogeochemical systems. This, too, is concealed by the logic of efficiency and is a sacrilege on a scale that we have no power to describe. We seem paralyzed by that fact, or perhaps strangely fascinated by it. Paradoxically, while we are causing death at the largest scale possible, we take ever greater pains to deny our own mortality. It is plausible that no previous culture has had greater difficulty coming to grips with death; our fears are magnified by our technology. We flirt with death as voyeurs, fascinated by the violence and death portrayed on film and television. Our children grow up playing violent video games. Risk incurred from the abuse of drugs and alcohol is widespread. A few participate in extreme sports but most of us drive carelessly and knowingly take many other risks. Our minds are populated with figures such as Hannibal Lector, Jason of Friday the Thirteenth fame, and any number of serial killers whose faces are featured on trading cards like sports figures. Death terrifies and fascinates us as it has no other people. Teenage boys, in particular, exhibit this tendency, but have few culturally approved and healthy ways in modern society to work through that stage of life to a stable maturity. How are we to overcome our need to deny death, and what would this mean for the larger society?

The psychologist, Ernest Becker, spent much of his life trying to understand why we deny death—what psychologists now call "terror management"—and how we do so. Denial of death takes many forms: "heroic transcendence, victory over evil for mankind as a whole, for unborn generations, consecration of one's existence to higher meanings."[8] Toward the end of his own life Becker concluded that "we are living the grotesque spectacle of the poisoning of the earth by the nineteenth-century hero system of unrestrained material production. This is perhaps the greatest and most pervasive evil to have emerged in all of history, and it may even eventually defeat all of mankind."[9] But he believed the causes of the evil to be ironic: "Men cause evil by wanting heroically to triumph over it, because man is a frightened animal who tries to triumph, an animal who will not admit his own insignificance."[10] The tragedy, he continues, "is that [evolution] created a limited animal with unlimited horizons."[11] Increasingly we manage our terror of mortality by trying to extend our power over nature through heroic feats of science, technology, and economic growth.

Life in an agrarian community, in contrast, is not heroic, nor is the denial of death a particularly useful response for farmers. Agrarian life, rather, requires a patient and painstaking accommodation to the realities of life and death in the effort to husband the health and long-term productivity of particular places. And this fact may help to explain some part of the rejection of family farming and agrarianism in our time. Good farming, as Wendell Berry describes it, does not lend itself to heroic projects, technological fantasies, or denial by consumption, carelessness, or great celebrity, requiring instead qualities of steadiness, hard work, neighborliness, practical competence, thrift, and perseverance. It is not farfetched to believe that we are now in full flight from such qualities, hoping to escape our bonds to mortality, time, work, nature, and our own nature. Neither is it far-fetched to believe that this flight has been aided and abetted by the same people and the same institutions that have corrupted our politics, economics, language, and education.

Possibilities

Wendell Berry describes two general organizing principles for society: one industrial, the other agrarian. The logic of industrial capitalism has brought us to a cul-de-sac. Instead of the limitless abundance promised, we face ruin on a global scale and as far into the future as the mind can comprehend. There are those who believe, nonetheless, that we might make a second and better industrial revolution. As proposed, that revolution requires no improvement in our politics, desires, economic thinking, connections to the land, and moral philosophy, only greater cleverness in how we handle materials so that we generate no waste and live on sunlight. There is much that is useful in this, but in the end it will founder on the shoals of hard reality and human recalcitrance. Why would people much enamored of wealth, convenience, and consumption decide to rouse themselves to heroic feats of cleverness, especially if the reward is not theirs? By what logic and by what means will capital rigged and outfitted for short-term exploitation of land and people be reformed to husband people as well as the natural capital of soils, forests, waters, and biological diversity over the long-term? In what way will people having defined themselves as consumers, and thereby diminished their role as a public, decide to work for a common good including that of nonhuman nature? I cannot imagine a system built on exploitation, consumption, growth, and uniformity—however cleverly managed—as anything other than a prelude to ruin.

However, to say that industrialism, even a smarter version of it, cannot be sustained is not to say that agrarianism will succeed. Darker possibilities are certainly imaginable. Perhaps agrarianism will prevail, as Churchill once said of democracy, only after we have tried everything else—if we have not ruined everything that really matters in the trying.

What, then, is the future of agrarianism? Is it possible, as Eric Freyfogle hopefully asserts, that even in a rapidly urbanizing world "agrarianism is again on the rise"?[12] If so, is it also possible for that rise to become a flood that recasts the industrial world in an agrarian mode? How might this happen? Few good social changes occur without hard work, organizing, and effective strategy. Agrarians are no strangers to the first, but are famous neither for organizing or thinking strategically. They are better known for their independence, self-reliance, and, yes, crankiness. The Vanderbilt Agrarians, for instance, having delivered themselves of their manifesto in 1930, mostly disappeared back into their various writing and academic endeavors and the world went on as before. The sustainable agriculture movement of the past three decades, for all of its accomplishments, still exists at the margin of our politics. The power of agribusiness, petrochemical companies, and the food industry seems undiminished.

✓ Still, I believe Freyfogle is onto something for reasons that Wendell Berry has explained in detail for nearly four decades: we have no better alternative. But that is not to say that agrarianism is inevitable everywhere or in any particular place indefinitely. To the contrary, the making of an agrarian world will require a great deal of thought, effort, political savvy, stamina, and orneriness. This is not about tinkering with "the system," but means a more fundamental change in how we relate to the land and to each other not as exploiters but as members of a community who intend to stay.

Agrarianism, as described by Berry, is no small, whittled-down philosophy for rural folks. It is rather a full-blown philosophy rooted in the realities of soil and nature as "the standard" by which we also come to judge much more. It is grounded in farming, but is larger still. The logic of agrarianism, in Berry's work, unfolds like a fractal through the divisions and incoherence of the modern world. It is, in his word, a "re-membering" of the wholeness and the Holiness of the creation. His is a philosophy that begins with place, soil, and farming, but is extended to include race, religion, sexuality, science, politics, wilderness, economics, world trade, food, foreign policy, and more. For the first time in the long history of agrarianism we have a philosophy that doesn't end at the farm gate with a description of the bucolic pleasures of tending to the soil. Berry's great achievement, I believe, is to describe eloquently and in great detail how our connections to soil, food, and agriculture extend through virtually everything else. He's given us a grounded philosophy of the wholeness of things with the admonition to "solve for pattern."

The pattern includes much more than farming, although that is the starting point. For agrarianism to work, it must have urban allies, urban farms, and urban restaurants patronized by people who love good food responsibly and artfully grown. It must have people who appreciate the pleasures of eating and who regard it, as Berry has said, as a political act. It must have farmers who regard themselves as trustees of the land that is to be passed on in health to future generations. It must have communities that value farms, farmland, and open spaces. It must have visionary and courageous policy makers who serve as trustees for our common wealth. It must have scientists, like Wes Jackson and his colleagues at the Land Institute, who will create the knowledge necessary for a twenty-first-century agrarianism. It must have bookkeepers that tell us the truth about wealth and its limits. It must have elders to remind us that we, the soil, and all that lives are part of the same ancient pattern, one and indivisible. This is only to say that an agrarian world requires a discerning public that understands that health, too, is indivisible.

This public cannot be willed into existence, it must be educated to regard itself as a public and to understand the connections between food and the health of the land, soils, and waters. But here's the rub: the practices, traditions, and memories of farming have been passed down from one generation to the next in the daily routines of living on the land. They have seldom been an important or effective part of any formal curriculum. To the contrary, schooling has mostly been thought of and defended as a way to escape the farm and to improve one's economic possibilities by becoming useful to the industrial economy. For agrarianism to succeed, I believe that this must change and, in fact, is changing. But much more will have to be done.

A public that understands the relationships between soil, forests, water, food, and health requires an educational system that equips students to comprehend systems and patterns. Every high-school graduate ought to understand the connections between the dead zone in the Gulf of Mexico, farm practices in the corn-soybean belt, the depletion of the Ogallala aquifer, oil wars, the rising tide of obesity, dying rural towns, urban sprawl, and antibiotic resistance. But this in turn would require a curriculum no longer organized exclusively by disciplines, nor one that rests on the assumption of human dominance over nature as a matter beyond debate. It is a curriculum that enables students to think "at right angles" to narrow disciplines, as Aldo Leopold once put it, and one that fosters ecological imagination. But that is a transformation well beyond what typically passes for educational reform.

At the earliest ages, education ought to do the work once done at home of connecting children to their places. School gardens and gardening could be a cornerstone of the daily experience of children. The Center for Ecoliteracy in Berkeley, for example, is helping to establish gardens in public schools throughout California as a way to improve cafeteria meals, teach biology, earn money from the sale of the surplus, and add to children's sense of connection and competence. The values of gardening are many; as an educational tool they can help to develop the ecological imagination of children in association with pleasurable activity. The same holds true at higher levels as well. For a dozen years I have taught a course in sustainable agriculture to students at Oberlin with mostly urban backgrounds. Many of those students have participated in the creation of a community-supported farm, restaurant, and health-food store. This strong interest here and on other campuses reflects a great desire to connect with the land and reform the food system along lines that fit agrarianism through and through.

Further, the buying power of schools, colleges, and universities ought to be used to support local farms and farmers. A dependable market for locally grown farm products can be an important stimulus to help establish sustainable agriculture. Students at California State University at Chico, for example, purchase T-shirts made from organically grown cotton to sell in the campus store. And there are more ambitious possibilities as well. Colleges might use a small portion of their assets to purchase farms that would otherwise be developed, leasing these back to young people wanting to farm but lacking the financial means to do so, thereby maintaining open space and protecting the local heritage, environment, and long-term values. Further, colleges and universities could provide a guaranteed market for the produce from such farms and help establish relationships with older farmers who could serve as mentors in the practical arts of agriculture. With some imagination, in other words, universities could help to stop urban sprawl and reestablish viable local farms.

And there is one other large possibility. The cornerstone of the industrial world rests on the availability of cheap fossil fuels and the belief that it is our right to burn them as we please. An agrarian world must be powered on contemporary sunshine. But in the present vacuum of leadership on climate policy, schools, colleges, and universities could lead in the transition to the solar age. To that end many colleges are beginning to develop plans to become climatically neutral in the next few decades through a combination of improved efficiency, buying "green power" from utilities, and the application of advanced technology such as photovoltaics, fuel cells, and wind turbines. The creation of a distributed energy system, similar to distributed computing, would reduce vulnerability to terrorism, eliminate emission of greenhouse gases, lower our balance of payments deficit, improve energy efficiency, and build a citizen-based energy system. It is no longer a question of technology, but one of leadership and vision.

There is serious work to do to elaborate and extend the agrarian idea and overcome the biases inherent in a curriculum organized around "upward mobility" and economic growth. Books such as this one can help, but the possibilities are many. Agrarianism could fail in the public marketplace because of the lack of coherent, well-articulated, and forcefully presented ideas, however true and important. Another Berry, Thomas Berry, calls all of this the "Great Work." Wendell Berry proposes that we aim to do great work in the minute particulars of living within our means as persons and as a people in the full awareness that the world is rich in possibilities. The question for all of us is what use we will make of those prophetic possibilities.

twelve

The Constitution of Nature

Turmoil in the Middle East, Africa, and South Asia has plunged the world into yet another era of nation building. The United States is engaged in the difficult task of reconstructing Afghanistan and Iraq purportedly along democratic lines. Beneath all of the rhetoric it is assumed that democracy is a useful model for severely conflicted Muslim countries with no experience of it and, further, that ours is an adequate framework in which to conduct the public business of any country in the twenty-first century. The first assumption has been challenged as premature or even naive.[1] But it is the second, and more important, of the two that I intend to question, in particular the constitutional framework within which our own politics occur.

The U.S. Constitution, ratified in 1788, reflects the opinions that originated in the Enlightenment era about many things, not the least of which is that ordinary people—within limits—are capable of self-governance. The document had the virtues of flexibility and ambiguity that have allowed it to frame U.S. political life from that time to our own, through civil war and the transition from an agrarian society to an industrial and technologically advanced behemoth. It has provided, as Robert Dahl notes, a model of sorts for more than one hundred other nations, but few have adopted its core assumptions about the actual organization of power.[2] In our own history the transition of the Constitution from "charter into scripture" did not occur until sometime in the late nineteenth century.[3] Since 1791 it has been amended seventeen times but without substantially altering the overall document. That fact alone suggests caution about changing something that has worked so well for so long.

Or has it? "Compared with other democratic countries," says Dahl the "performance [of the U.S. Constitution] appears, on balance, to be mediocre at best."[4] His judgment is based on political criteria, but there are other and broader ways by which we might judge the Constitution. How well, for example, has it worked as a framework for protecting the waters, land, forests, soils, wildlife, and ecological integrity of the United States? A thorough reading of the evidence indicates serious decline in virtually every category.[5] Dead zones, extinctions, toxic pollution, soil erosion, radioactivity, urban sprawl, smog, industrial sacrifice areas, and changing climate are the ecological hallmarks of economic development in the United States. But do such things reflect failures of the Constitution or broader failures in our political system, or some combination of the two?

Such questions would not have been intelligible to the framers. For them the conquest of nature by science and technology was an unmixed blessing. In our time, we can see the limits of nature, some say its end. We know what they could not have known: that nature is an intricate web of causes and effects often widely separated in space and time, and that small changes can have very large effects. We know, too, that what we mean by nature is complicated by our being bound up in it in ways that are hard to fathom. And we know, or ought to know, that we could bring it and ourselves crashing down gradually or quickly. The framers of the U.S. Constitution could not have foreseen this, although James Madison and Thomas Jefferson came to believe that the experiment with democracy might not last beyond the time of cheap land.[6] We, however, know the ecological history of the intervening years and, arguably, have a better capacity to comprehend the future.[7] All of this is to say that we can judge the Constitution and the political life it fostered in an ecological perspective that the framers did not have. From this vantage point, three issues are particularly important: the inclusiveness of constitutional protection, the applicability of due process, and the fragmentation of political power.

1. Inclusiveness. Although they began with the words "We the People," the framers did not include women, Native Americans, or African Americans. The omissions were rectified by the thirteenth, fourteenth, fifteenth, nineteenth, and twenty-fourth amendments. But no such protection has yet been granted to future generations, even though we know that the decisions and actions of the present generation cast a long shadow on their prospects in ways that could not have been known in the eighteenth century. Of the founders, Jefferson is notable for his worries about the intergenerational effects of debt, but no one could have known about intergenerational ecological debt and such things as the extinction of species, climatic change, and toxic pollution. "We the People" meant we the present generation, with the caveat that the framers intended to "secure the blessings of liberty to ourselves and our posterity." To do so meant getting the framework issues right enough to balance interests, avoid the tyranny of either minority or majority, provide democratic representation, create national institutions, and establish a credit-worthy government. But the framers placed no restrictions on the rights of the living relative to those of subsequent generations. It would be a mistake, however, to infer that the framers had no further regard for posterity. To the contrary, I think they did but assumed that obligations to the future had been discharged by the creation of a durable national government. Many now believe that future generations need more explicit protection.

In 1986 the Supreme Court of the Philippines, for example, upheld the standing of children to litigate in order to stop deforestation on behalf of future generations' rights to "a balanced and healthy ecology." To acknowledge standing, the Court drew from no specific textual reference saying only that "these basic rights need not even be written in the Constitution for they are assumed to exist from the inception of humankind."[8] The proper question, then, is not whether succeeding generations have legitimate rights to a balanced and healthy ecology, but how those rights might be determined and enforced in the present. But given the intergenerational reach of technology, the issues go much past the protection of resources. Do our descendents, for example, have a legitimate claim to a genetic heritage stable within definable limits?[9] Ought their interests to be weighed in decisions, say, about genetic enhancement of human intelligence and extension of the human lifespan that would become permanent features or perhaps even the beginnings of a new species? If so, how would we know their preferences or best interests, a different thing? Should their probable wishes or interests be considered in other decisions having to do with the development of nanotechnologies and artificial intelligence that might diminish their prospects or foreclose them altogether? If such rights are extended to future generations, who will speak for them and how will those rights be honored in practice? Regarding the former, there are instructive precedents in trusteeship and court-appointed guardians for those unable to defend their own interests. And there are a variety of public-policy tools to protect future generations, including prices that include true ecological costs, depletion quotas or severance taxes that slow the drawdown of resources, taxes on pollution, land trusts, and the police power of the state through regulation. Whatever difficulties we may encounter in applying these or other methods should be not be used to override the fact that no good argument can be made for the right of one generation to deprive subsequent generations of the ecological requisites necessary to pursue life, liberty, and property.

Going further, the Constitution deals solely with humans and their affairs, which is to say that it is purely anthropocentric. But there is a broader way to think about constitutions. French sociologist Bruno Latour, for one, proposes that we distinguish between "the full constitution" and "the constitution of jurists."[10] The former includes the unstated assumptions underlying the latter and accounts for "the distribution of powers among human beings, gods, non humans; the procedures for reaching agreements; the connections between religion and power; ancestors; cosmology; property rights; plant and animal taxonomies."[11] This larger constitution "defines humans and nonhumans, their properties and their relations, their abilities and their groupings."[12] This is, I think, what Aldo Leopold had in mind when he described humans as "plain members and citizens of the land-community."[13] But nowhere in the U.S. Constitution are the other members of the land community acknowledged. As Latour notes, the framers assumed that nature and society were entirely separate and that humans were "free to reconstruct [nature] artificially."[14] Lacking any constitutional recognition or protection, nature was there for the taking, and it was taken. In the words of Howard Mumford Jones,

[There was a continent to ravage [and Americans took a] fierce, adolescent joy in smashing things—in stripping mountains to get at the ore, laying forests waste for their better timber, plowing up the plains whether normal crops could grow on them or not, slaughtering millions of bison . . . scarifying whole counties with the poisonous fumes of smelters, polluting rivers with sludge from oil wells, slaughterhouse, and city sewage . . . [15]

If the Constitution could, in time, be broadened to rectify past human wrongs through the amendments that extended the rights of citizenship to African Americans and women, no such thing has been done relative to the members of the land community. And some are still caught up in the adolescent joy of smashing things.

Latour proposes "a different democracy . . . [one] extended to things."[16] Aldo Leopold similarly believed that inclusion of "soils, waters, plants, and animals, or collectively: the land" in our definition of community was both "an evolutionary possibility and an ecological necessity."[17] Leopold never wrote about the legal implications of this idea, assuming that the beginning point for law and policy was first to enlarge the boundaries of ethical consideration and law would someday follow. If and when it does there are difficult issues to resolve about how rights and duties pertain across species boundaries. Is it logical or practical to include the rights of species? Ought we to consider the rights of ecosystems, as Leopold proposed, and what does this mean? How are we to discern the interests of nonhuman entities, or consider ourselves obliged when reciprocity is not possible? If these issues could be decided affirmatively, how might they be integrated into our complicated systems of politics and jurisprudence?

Again, complexities should not be used as an excuse to dismiss the issues and thereby the possibilities of extending constitutional protections in important and novel ways. Leopold believed that an ecological comprehension of our own self-interest would lead us, in time, to see that our well-being was inextricably tied to the health of the land community. Said differently, human interests and the efficacy of law would be markedly diminished in a ruined ecological system. What could it possibly mean for Americans to have the rights guaranteed in the Constitution in a land with a diminished biota, despoiled landscapes, polluted air and water, little topsoil, ravaged forests, and a climate growing more severe decade by decade? Rights in such conditions would be no better than having legal entitlement to an apartment in a demolished building.

2. *Due Process.* The fourth amendment protects "the right of people to be secure in their persons, houses, papers, and effects." Yet these people so secured have dozens or hundreds of chemicals in their bloodstream and fatty tissues from exposure to the thousands of chemicals in our food, air, water, and materials.[18] The privacy of the body has been invaded mostly without our knowledge or permission, and with little accountability by those responsible. The ubiquity of pollution means that responsibility is difficult to ascertain; and it is still more difficult to determine which of hundreds or thousands of chemicals, mixing in ways beyond our comprehension, caused exactly what pathology. Our knowledge of such things is inescapably general. We know that some of these substances, singly or in combination, undermine health, reproductive potential, intelligence, ability to concentrate, and emotional stability hence the capacity to pursue and experience life, liberty, and happiness. But it is nearly impossible to know exactly which ones, in what combinations, and at what specific levels. We know that children are more vulnerable to chemicals and heavy metals than adults and that some physical and mental effects are permanent. But we cannot know in advance which children are most susceptible. We know, however, that the liberty of some to make and disperse toxic chemicals and heavy metals conflicts with the rights and liberties of those exposed. In some cases the effects will manifest far into the future, placing perpetrators beyond the reach of law and leaving their victims without remedy. What, then, does it mean that we cannot "be deprived of life, liberty, or property," including property of the body, without "due process of law" as stated in both the fifth and fourteenth amendments?

The framers could not have known about carcinogenic, mutagenic, or endocrine-disrupting substances, or radioactivity, but we do. For many toxic substances we know that there appears to be no safe threshold of exposure. Chemicals that disrupt the endocrine system do their work in parts per billion, wreaking havoc on the development and immune system of children. Had they known what we now know about the ubiquity of chemicals and their effects, would the framers have extended the protections of due process to include the fundamental right of bodily integrity? And should such protections be extended more broadly to include deprivation of other ecologically grounded requisites of life and liberty?

E. O. Wilson, for example, describes our affinity for nature as "biophilia," which he defines as an innate "urge to affiliate with other forms of life."[19] He writes that "we are human in good part because of the particular way we affiliate with other organisms."[20] Nature, then, is not something "out there," but rather something that has been inscribed in us, and after several million years of evolution it would be surprising were it otherwise. Environmental psychologists similarly describe nature as experienced in childhood as a kind of substrate of our consciousness and emotions. Could it be that the disruption of natural processes diminishes the possibility of affiliation with nature? Does ugliness, in all of its modern forms, diminish the human psyche and thereby the capacity for biophilia? Could it be that the diminished possibility for affiliation with a healthy nature reduces the quality of life? A growing body of scientific research suggests that this chain of reasoning is more than just plausible. If so, the constitutional protections of due process ought to be broadened someday to protect those aspects of life and liberty uniquely and irrevocably grounded in the experience of nature.

3. Fragmented Power. The framers created a system aimed to check ambition, competing interests, and the possibility of tyranny from a highly centralized government. To these ends, the Constitution divides power between the legislative, executive, and judicial branches and further between federal and state governments. Over time the fragmentation of government powers has increased with the growth of federal agencies, departments, and programs. The result is that, relative to environmental policy, the right hand of government often knows not what the left hand is up to. The Department of Commerce, for example, promotes economic expansion while the Environmental Protection Agency is expected to clean up the resulting messes. The Department of Energy promotes an energy plan with more nuclear power plants that, were it implemented, the Department of Defense could not conceivably defend from terrorists. The system of checks and balances, furthermore, limits the ability of the federal government to anticipate, plan, and respond to systemic problems or better yet, to avoid them altogether. But the larger problem is the mismatch between the way nature works in highly connected and interactive ecosystems and the fragmentation of powers built into the Constitution. Nature is a unified mosaic of ecosystems, functions, and processes. Government, on the other hand, was conceived by the founders as a limited and fractured enterprise.

In the intervening years, government programs have grown as disjointed and incremental responses intended to solve particular problems. Not infrequently, a solution to one problem becomes the cause of later problems. The Clean Air Act of 1970, for example, required scrubbing power plant emissions, but the substances so removed were deposited on land and thus became a land-use problem. The effect, in this and other cases, has been a kind of shell game by which problems are not solved but moved from air, to water, to land and back again. Governments commonly deal with the coefficients of problems, not with the system that created the problems in the first place. Reduced automobile pollution is a worthy goal, but the problem is systemic, having to do with the lack of anything like an intelligent transportation system that would include trains, bike trails, walking paths, and highways. Environmental laws seldom prevent or solve environmental problems. At best they render them somewhat more manageable, while providing fertile ground for legal wrangling over the permissible rates by which the citizenry is poisoned and the land degraded.

The intent of the framers to limit and divide power, in other words, has become an impediment to the creation of effective environmental policy. "The Madisonian model," according to Steven Kelman, "make[s] it more difficult to produce government action of *any* sort."[21] Relative to environmental matters and the rights of future generations, gridlock is now *the* default setting of U.S. government. Consequently, since the 1970s there has been virtually no advance in our ability to protect or enhance environmental quality. At best, air and water quality are in a holding pattern while other, and more serious, problems worsen.

II

Even though "it is time—long past time—to invigorate and greatly widen the critical examination of the Constitution and its shortcomings," says Robert Dahl, "public discussion that penetrates beyond the Constitution as a national icon is virtually nonexistent."[22] Dahl believes the Constitution to be insufficiently democratic. As presently interpreted, it is also deficient in ecological terms and these are, I think, related problems. The framers' worldviews were a complicated mosaic of European and Scottish philosophy, agrarianism, frontier practicality, and native American wisdom. And the men themselves were businessmen with an eye to pecuniary advantage, as Charles Beard established long ago.[23] They had, as Dahl and others note, mixed opinions about democracy. But they did not know and could not have known how the world works as an ecological system and that the unfettered advance of technology would someday cast a dark shadow on a distant posterity. The question is whether that lack can be remedied by law, constitutional amendment, broader political change, or by some combination of the three.

The most notable example of a legislative remedy was the

National Environmental Policy Act of 1969 intended "to improve and coordinate Federal plans, functions, and programs . . . to the end that the nation may fulfill the responsibilities of each generation as trustee of the environment for succeeding generations." NEPA is an eloquent statement of a national environmental policy that had and still has great potential. The act mandated environmental impact statements for "federal actions significantly affecting the quality of the human environment." But it has foundered, in the opinion of its principal author, on the shoals of presidential indifference, judicial misinterpretation, public apathy, broad incomprehension of the environment, and the lack of "a great unifying goal," none of which are specifically constitutional matters.[24] Much of the same can be said of the effectiveness of the Endangered Species Act of 1973 that also required an ecologically literate congress and executive and an informed public. NEPA notwithstanding, the United States has no effective environmental policy and none whatsoever relative to energy use, land use, transportation, or agriculture. Instead we have a hodgepodge of poorly enforced laws, regulations, and practices, some of which work at cross-purposes, and no one of which prevents environmental degradation in the first place. Despite the intentions of Congress, environmental laws and regulations have been watered down for the convenience of major economic interests. NEPA did not end the fragmentation of power established in the Constitution.

Regarding the second approach, there have been three attempts (1967, 1968, and 1970) to amend the Constitution in order to grant rights to a healthy environment by law. But is it necessary to amend the Constitution to do so? Legal scholar Bruce Ledewitz believes not. "There is," he writes, "no impediment in the political Constitution to the derivation of expansive constitutional rights particularly at a time in which the future of humankind may be at stake."[25] The obstacles, in his view, are not problems of the Constitution or the intent of the founders, but rather the embarrassing ecological obsolescence of U.S. constitutional law, a legal community ignorant of the scale of environmental problems, and the possibility that "the current generation may prefer its own wealth and convenience over that of future generations," which is a political problem.[26] But despite the power of the idea and the urgency of the situation, Ledewitz concludes that "the time is not ripe" for expanding the scope of the law or passing a constitutional amendment. In his view the problem is fundamentally political and requires "a revitalization of our democracy."[27] And that leads to a more complicated set of issues.

III

The founders' generation fought to overthrow the tyranny of the British monarchy, but tyranny in our time is far more pervasive and oppressive in two respects. First, moneyed interests in the form of corporations have acquired an undeserved advantage, a stranglehold as it were, over the public interest. The public is losing control over much of the public commons: capital, information, airwaves, land, health care, employment, genetic information, and, if the acolytes of free trade have their way, the power to control our own economic affairs.[28] Further, we the people are excluded from fundamental decisions about war and peace, nuclear weapons policy, and the growing number of decisions about technology in which there is some probability of irretrievable disaster. Once, we became much exercised about "taxation without representation," but the present reality is more akin to "extermination without representation."

Second, tyranny is now intergenerational and to a great extent irrevocable and is therefore beyond remedy. The effects of climate change, loss of species, destruction of ecosystems, and tropical deforestation are global, threaten to erode the ecological foundations of civilized societies, and are for all practical purposes permanent. Looming on the horizon are technologies that, once deployed, could fundamentally and irrevocably alter what it means to be human and change the role of humankind in a world of machines designed to be smarter than people and capable of self-replication. In other words, the global environmental effects of the industrial-era will cast a long shadow on future generations everywhere, for all time. This tyranny will be imposed by ecological degradation, genetic pollution, destructive and uncontrollable technology, and worsening climatic conditions. If it is to be avoided, the present generation must restrain its appetites and behavior. Our time is far more portentous than that of the framers' and calls for a more thorough consideration of law, democracy, rights, and the public trust relative to the human prospect.

Neither constitutional amendment nor law alone can solve what is inherently a political problem. But "a bankrupt politics of sideshow issues and elusive leadership that ignores the burning social needs of the day is not a politics that inspires citizens to action."[29] And citizen apathy is greatly fortified by a media given to report the scandalous and sensational, not issues of real substance. We are rather like the lost traveler told by the mountaineer that "you can't get there from here." Or can we?

The changes that must be made are resonant with much of our history, best values, and notions of common sense. There are two keystone principles. One requires that we act conservatively in cases where the risks of widespread, severe, and irreversible harm are high or simply unknown.[30] Such precaution is as commonplace in daily affairs as it seems radical in the realm of public policy. As individuals we buy insurance, have annual physical exams, and wear seatbelts, which is to say that we exercise caution for reasons so obvious as to require no explanation. In medicine the principle of precaution is widely accepted in the words "first do no harm." In public policy we must acknowledge a comparable logic in situations in which the risks may be catastrophic and our ignorance far exceeds our knowledge. It is one thing for individuals to incur risks to themselves and another thing entirely for some few to risk the welfare of the many, including those who have no say in the matter. The present situation privileges the rights of the elite who cannot be held accountable if and when things turn out badly. As it stands, the benefits of risk are in effect privatized while the risks are socialized across generational lines, and this, by any decent reckoning, is unfair.

The second principle is grounded in our ancient concepts of rights. If, indeed, "all men [*including those yet to live*] are created equal, that they are endowed by their Creator with certain unalienable rights, that among these are Life, Liberty, and the Pursuit of Happiness," then *no generation has license to diminish the unalienable rights of subsequent generations by changing the biogeochemical systems of Earth or impairing the stability, integrity, and beauty of biotic systems, the consequences of which are a form of intergenerational tyranny.* Ignorance can no longer serve as a good or plausible defense for actions that compromise the legitimate rights of present and future generations. Accordingly, a truly conservative *and* revolutionary reading of the U.S. Constitution would build on the idea that we are trustees poised between our forebears and our posterity. In trust we are obliged by decency, fairness, justice, and affection to protect, preserve, and honor the ecological prospects of existing life and that yet to be. Without that guarantee other purely legal rights can have little meaning. It is absurd to believe that the framers, seven generations ago, would have wished us to preserve the letter of the Constitution of 1788 while permitting the destruction of the very ground on which that document and life itself depend.

I do not think we are as stuck as some would have it. First, across the political spectrum there is substantial and broad agreement about the sanctity of life shared, for example, by those who oppose abortion and by those who aim to protect species and landscapes. What at first appears as an irreconcilable difference is rooted in a common commitment to protect life and the conditions that allow it to flourish. That commonality, were it tapped, constitutes a potent political force across what seem to be hard and fast political divisions. There are other principles that transcend right and left, including the Public Trust Doctrine, holding that the public good ought to take precedence over private gain. This, too, is widely accepted by the public, if not by those who gain much by the abuse of private gain. We do not lack for common ground, but rather the kind of leadership that is capable of articulating the values that unite us.

Second, the time has come for an ecological enlightenment in law schools and in the courts. The law in all of its forms has many ecological implications that ripple outward in space and time. Those practicing law and those charged with its adjudication ought to be aware of those possibilities and the science by which such potential consequences are framed and understood. Ignorance of ecology by lawyers and jurists is no longer excusable as something pertaining to a separate and unrelated realm. And given the close relationship between law and politics, the effects of greater ecological understanding by the legal profession will eventually have great impact on our politics as well.

Third, it is time for bold action to head off the worst of what may lie ahead, beginning with a Constitutional amendment guaranteeing the right to a healthy environment. If not now, when? The last such attempt occurred in 1970, but since that time public awareness of the scale, scope, and duration of the ecological crisis has grown considerably. Would such an initiative be controversial? Certainly, but less than one might fear. Let those who oppose the peoples' rights to clean air, clean water, open space, and healthy ecosystems stand up and say so. When they do, they will lose. Opinion surveys over three decades consistently show a large majority in favor of environmental quality, clear air, limits to sprawl, energy efficiency, renewable energy, and controls on pollution. But the machinery that ostensibly connects public opinion with public policy is broken.

The effort to establish and pass a constitutional amendment would have salutary effects. It would focus what is now a scattered debate on the essentials of our relationship to our children and theirs. It would end two decades of stalemate on environmental policy. It would exert a steady gravitational pull toward remedy and reconciliation of human interests and ecological realities. The full effects of the thirteenth, fourteenth, and fifteenth amendments, for example, were not felt until after the civil rights legislation of 1964 and 1965, but the power of the law, if dormant, was never extinguished. The acknowledgement of the rights to a healthy environment now and for those yet to live would clarify necessary changes in policy having to do with taxes, prices, public expenditures, the proper control of corporations, and the directions of technology.

IV

The U.S. Constitution is not just words on paper. It is a living, evolving document. Its great virtue is its "extraordinary capacity for self-revision."[31] It is "an open and revolutionary document," as Ledewitz reminds us, and "need not be interpreted to stand mute while the environment and the interests of the future are sacrificed."[32] It is time for our understanding of that document to be reconciled with our knowledge of both natural systems and our growing awareness of obligations and rights that extends broadly throughout the community of life and outward in time as far as the mind dares to imagine. And for those intending to aggressively spread the U.S. version of democracy far and wide, it would be good were our example one that preserved a habitable earth on behalf of those yet to be born.

thirteen

Imagine a World:
The Education of Our Leaders

The events of 9/11 highlighted the obvious fact that actions taken by one nation, people, religion, or corporation ripple throughout the entire world, but those most affected seldom have any vote or voice and future generations, none at all. Pollution from the use of coal in China falls out over the United States and Canada. Carbon dioxide emissions from U.S. power plants reduces rainfall in the Sahel. Radioactivity from Chernobyl is detectable virtually everywhere. Broadcast by television and print media, Western-style consumerism has become the goal of most people everywhere without much thought or foresight. Fanaticism from the right and the left sets in motion global forces that we see only in hindsight. Once separate, the human family is fast becoming one family.

Divided by nationality, ethnicity, religion, wealth, and power, we are nonetheless joined by evolution, ecology, morality, and increasingly by sheer necessity.

We are still governed, however, as if we exist in separate worlds. Never has the need for genuine leadership been greater, and seldom has it been less evident. The human family cannot survive another century of vacillating leaders such as those who allowed the world to drift into World War I, or monsters such as Adolf Hitler, Joseph Stalin, Pol Pot, Mao Tse-tung, or petty but dangerous tyrants like Idi Amin and Saddam Hussein. We cannot be ruled by ignorant, malicious, greedy, incompetent, and shortsighted people and expect things to turn out well. If we are to navigate the challenges of the decades ahead—what E. O. Wilson calls "the bottleneck"— we will need leaders of great stature, clarity of mind, spiritual depth, courage, and vision. We need leaders who see patterns that connect us across the divisions of culture, religion, geography, and time. We need leadership that draws us together to resolve conflicts, move quickly from fossil fuels to solar power, reverse global environmental deterioration, and empower us to provide shelter, food, medical care, decent livelihood, and education for everyone. We need leadership that is capable of energizing genuine commitment to old and venerable traditions as well as new visions for a global civilization that preserves and honors local cultures, economies, and knowledge.

But even in purportedly democratic countries citizens have little real say over those who govern us and none at all over those who rise to power elsewhere. We assume that the emergence of real leadership is a random occurrence and hope that the right person(s) would emerge at just the right place and time. But in business, education, and the nonprofit sectors, we know that chance is not good enough and so we train leaders in the arts and science of leadership. We test prospective drivers' knowledge of the rules of the road before granting them a license, but political leaders need only prove that they are beneficial for the wealthy, look good on television, and are masters of the arts of public manipulation.

Imagine a world, however, in which those who purport to lead us first make a pilgrimage to ground zero at Hiroshima and publicly pledge "never again." Imagine a world in which those who purport to lead us go to Auschwitz and the Killing Fields and pledge publicly "never again." Imagine a world in which leaders go to Bhopal and say to the victims, "We are truly sorry. This will never happen again, anywhere." Imagine, too, those pilgrim leaders going to sites where love, kindness, forgiveness, sacrifice, compassion, wisdom, ingenuity, and foresight have been evident: Assisi, the home of Saint Francis; Le Chambon, where French villagers acted to save Jews during the Nazi occupation; a shelter for the homeless in New York; the city of Curitiba in Brazil; the research center of Las Gaviotas in Colombia; Amish country; perhaps a cohousing project in the Netherlands; and Auroville, India.

Imagine a time in which those purporting to lead us first describe publicly how they propose to help forge a decent and sustainable path out of the social and ecological catastrophes looming ahead. The speech would be both visionary and specific. It could have the pathos of Pericles' "Funeral Oration," the kindness of Saint Francis's "Sermon to the Birds," the power and concision of Lincoln's Gettysburg Address, the defiance of Churchill's "Blood, Sweat, and Tears," or that of a different sort in Gandhi's speech, "Non Cooperation," or the scope of vision in Martin Luther King's "I Have a Dream." The point is to give each potential leader an opportunity to think as widely and deeply as possible about the large issues on the human agenda and to announce themselves to all of those who will be affected by their decisions. Refusal to do so would announce darker possibilities.

Imagine a world in which those who purport to lead us help identify places around the world degraded by human actions and help initiate their restoration. Some projects might take as long as one thousand years to restore: the Aral

Sea, the ecology of the Harrapan region in India, the forests of Lebanon, soil fertility in the Middle East, the Chesapeake Bay, the North Atlantic cod fishery—the possibilities are many. Imagine a world in which those who intend to lead help lift our sights above the daily crisis to the far horizon of what could be.

Imagine a world in which we expect leaders to be knowledgeable people who meet each year not to talk about economic growth, but about ecological and human health—a more complicated and pressing subject. Imagine a world in which those who purport to lead had actually read widely and thought deeply about the directions of technology, suffering, nature, agriculture, ethics, political philosophy, and the human future. Imagine leaders with minds informed through conversations with the wisest thinkers of our time such as Wendell Berry, Jane Goodall, Satish Kumar, and Helena Norberg-Hodge.

Oddly, we require more of prospective auto drivers than we do of our leaders. The former at least must pass a test about the rules of the road, but leaders' understanding of leadership is untested until they are already in the driver's seat. But imagine a time in which those who purport to lead us would have to understand fundamentals such as how the Earth works as a physical system, the state of the planet, emerging solar technologies, policies necessary for sustainability, economics suitable for a small planet, ecological design, and techniques of conflict resolution. Imagine a world in which leaders spend time in homeless shelters, barrios, and refugee camps.

Imagine, further, a world in which those who purport to lead us would be expected to have what Daniel Goleman calls "emotional intelligence."[1] For good reasons we penalize drunk drivers. The same should be true of those intoxicated by ego, power, and ideology. Once in power, a considerable fraction cannot join their emotional lives with the practice of power in any healthy way, and a few become pathological. We should not ask less of our leaders than we do of drivers.

"Realists" will dismiss the idea of better leadership as muddleheaded. Some will see in it some global conspiracy or another. Prospective leaders will profess sympathy but say that they do not have the time to improve themselves further. And those least qualified to lead will pay no attention at all. But it is not up to any of them to prescribe for us. We are now citizens of the Earth joined in a common enterprise with many variations. We have every right to insist that those who purport to lead us be worthy of the task. Imagine such a time!

fourteen

Postscript: The Hour before Dawn

Recently I participated in a conference to assess the "State of the World." I was sixth on the list of speakers over three days, each of whom presented mostly well-documented and plausible bad news ranging from global famine to abrupt climate change to worldwide terrorism or all of the above. Gloom settled on the assembled like a dark cloud. I had intended to offer more of the same, but decided enough was enough. On the spur of the moment I began to list the legitimate reasons we have for optimism. Hope isn't the same thing as the wishful thinking because it recognizes reality for what it is and proceeds in faith and creativity to better possibilities. Hopefulness is predicated on our ability to choose—that we are not fated to end with a whimper or a bang. On the contrary, we are capable of love, foresight, altruism, sacrifice, and nobility. In hope and faith we are called to that side of our nature in the full awareness of our darker side. So, what are the reasons for genuine hope? I offer ten.

First, we have better ideas than they do. For thirty years or longer we environmentalists have been right on the big issues. Not always, but mostly. Rachel Carson was right about the effects of DDT and similar chemicals in 1962. Paul and Anne Ehrlich were right in 1968 about the possibilities for famine and ecological collapse. Presently 1 billion people are malnourished and some 30,000 or more die each day of malnutrition related diseases. Whole ecologies have collapsed in places like Haiti, Ethiopia, China, and elsewhere. The authors of the much maligned *Limits to Growth* were mostly right in 1972. There are real limits to what we can do, beginning with overloading the ability of the Earth to absorb our wastes. E. F. Schumacher was right about the limits to scale and the need for "appropriately scaled" technology. Amory Lovins was right in 1976 about the potential for greater energy efficiency and renewable energy sources. We have come partway down the road he described against the determined opposition of the fossil-fuel industries and electric utilities. Wendell Berry's indictment of the U.S. agricultural system remains the most cogent description of a massive failure of farming subsidized both by federal spending and by the natural largess of North America. And, in different ways, Randall Arendt, Jane Jacobs, Paul Hawken, Vaclav Havel, Jim Hightower, Wes Jackson, Bill McDonough, Ian McHarg, Vandana Shiva, John and Nancy Todd, Paul Wellstone, E. O. Wilson, and many, many others are right about better possibilities than those in prospect. It is not possible to organize the public business for long around hatred, fear, and resentment. There is some steady gravitational pull in the universe toward higher things.

Second, there are more of us than there are of them. Public opinion polls show determined majorities over three decades in favor of clean air, clean water, open spaces, preservation of species, climate stability, less traffic congestion, and solar energy. Such things are merely common sense and no good case can be made to the contrary. There is no mandate to repeal the gains of the twentieth century. But, as extremists of all kinds know, it is always possible to confuse, muddy the water, and distort reality—but only for so long. Our job is to educate, inform accurately, and help the public understand how to see the truth and discern large patterns of cause and effect. Or as Amory Lovins puts it, there is "faith, hope, and clarity, but the greatest of these is clarity."[1]

Third, there is the growing power of world opinion. The United States is now regarded by many around the world as a rogue nation engaging in state terrorism. But there are forces that will counter our arrogance and overreach. The ecological enlightenment, for one, has now grown to a global force multiplied by the Internet. How else but the Internet to explain the 600 million people who actively protested the onset of the war in Iraq? No matter the issue, there is a surge in public opinion in favor of a decent, peaceful, and sustainable world. I do not think that this tidal wave can be stopped by any nation or any amount of military power. Indeed it will feed on the excesses of the United States.

Fourth, an economy organized around the convenience of the top 5 percent cannot be maintained for long. Tax cuts for the hugely wealthy, rising deficits, and militarization of the economy is, and has always been, a recipe for disaster. Such an economy will finally end in permanent depression, revolution, or perhaps, with an outbreak of sanity. And there are better ideas for a truly prosperous economy waiting in the wings. We do not have to rob the world and steal from our children to live well. By a similar logic the organization of the global economy by the International Monetary Fund, World Bank, and the World Trade Organization cannot be sustained. It is too closed, too corrupt, too destructive, and too shortsighted to persevere. What we don't know is how it will end, whether in mass uprisings, collapse, thoroughgoing reform or by some combination of these.

Fifth, the facts are on our side. The extremists now in power believe that they can, rather like Stalin, match science to their personal predilections. It did not work very well for Stalin and it will work no better for them. They are certainly entitled to their opinions, but in matters of public policy they have no right to tailor the facts to fit their opinions. It is a fact that we are now changing the climate and that this may lead to disaster. It is a fact that we are driving thousands of species toward extinction, unraveling God's creation as it were. It is a fact that we are losing soil faster than it can be regenerated and thereby jeopardizing future food security. It is a fact that toxic pollution is now global and undermines both human and ecological health. It is a fact that all oceans and all fisheries are in peril. It is a fact that forests roughly the size of Scotland disappear each year. And the fact is that a third of humankind live at or below the point of decency. These are all well-known and well documented. So, too, are the technological possibilities and public policies that lead us in better directions.

Sixth, our technology is better than theirs. They've chosen to run the flag up the pole of nuclear energy, more fossil-fuel power plants, more oil wells, more coal mines, more tax breaks for Humvees, more air pollution, and more ecological destruction, to say nothing of smarter bombs and Star Wars technology. They cannot do such things for long without bringing about economic ruin, endless wars, more terror, political turmoil, isolation, and finally, ecological collapse. In the meantime there is a revolution underway built around the kinds of technology that power space-shuttle craft and that is now being applied to commercial buildings, houses, and cars. It is a revolution that will take us toward a distributed energy system based on efficiency and progress in photovoltaics, fuel cells, wind power, and micro turbines.[2] It cannot be stopped, but it can be slowed by shortsightedness driven by greed.

Seventh, the course we are now on runs counter to our history and to our best traditions, some of which are in need of serious repair. At our best we are a people defined by documents such as the Declaration of Independence, the Constitution, and the Gettysburg Address. We do not have to be a rogue nation given to secretly arranged preemptive wars and assassinations. We are a better people than that. The fact that the historical record diverges so sharply in recent decades from our higher values says much about the role of secrecy in our national life, the profitability of what President Eisenhower deemed a "military-industrial complex," and the cynical manipulation of patriotism.

Eighth, the world is more complicated than the neocons and the new imperialists would have it. Women are mobilizing. The Internet is connecting a global citizenry. Information is more available to those wishing to find it. There are more wild cards than ever before—which is to say the world cannot be controlled from the center—and no amount of military power can change that central fact. Imperialism is an ancient dream, a fool's errand really, that is no longer possible in what Jonathan Schell has called "the unconquerable world."[3] Add to this the fact that we live in an ironic and paradoxical world that mocks controllers and dominators of all kinds.

Ninth, there is a global spiritual revolution underway the likes of which we've not seen before.[4] People across the major faith traditions are organizing, talking, thinking, singing, chanting, and praying. There is power being unleashed and it transcends any one religion and any one nation. And despite differences, there is a lot of common ground around an agenda of peace, nonviolence, fairness, protection of communities, restoration of degraded places, ecological sustainability, an extended view of human rights as well as the rights of species and nature, and least, the rights of our children and those yet to live on Earth. Said differently, it is not possible for long to organize our affairs around greed, illusion, and ill will.

We are called to higher things. And in silence one can hear the birth pains of a new order of things . . . a new enlightenment.

Ten . . . speaking of spirituality, we have reason to think that God is on our side. Why? God, who apparently has a sense of humor, reportedly recalled for a time Rush Limbaugh's hearing, a seldom used faculty. And God will take back all unused faculties, among them humor, wisdom, creativity, foresight, and charity. These are the faculties that will take us to a different world—not utopia, but a far better world than that in prospect. The race has never been just to the swift, nor the battle to the merely strong (Ecclesiastes, 9:11). The better angels of our nature will prevail, and that is solid ground for hope.

The Education of Power

The person on the other end of the line was a well-known southern Republican. He was calling to ask me to join a group aiming to improve the environmental policies of the White House. The leaders of the group had approached Karl Rove asking for a meeting with senior administration officials to that end. Somewhat taken aback, I asked "why me?" "David," he responded, "you are known as a sane environmentalist." I'd been called worse, but offhand could not say when. Without knowing what I was getting in to, I joined.

That evening I called my ninety-four-year-old mother in Charlotte, North Carolina, a lifelong conservative Republican prone to vote for Jesse Helms (once a matter of family concern), to tell her I'd been invited to meet with senior administration officials. I had intended to assure her that my life was not totally wasted as an unrepentant environmentalist. There was a long pause on the other end of the line. "Well, that's mighty nice," she said in the sweetest southern drawl ever, "but why did they ask you?" "Mom," I said, "they think I'm a sane environmentalist." Another long pause, followed by, "Well, honey, they just don't know yuh like I know yuh."

The meeting, scheduled for September 2001, was interrupted by the events of 9/11. It took place a month later on October 11. For the nearly three months preceding the meeting, fifteen of us had drafted a forty-two-page paper to be given to White House officials that were to include, in addition to Karl Rove, the vice president, the secretary of the Department of the Interior, and the head of the Environmental Protection Agency, all of whom were to attend the meeting. Hunter Lovins, cofounder of the Rocky Mountain Institute, and I were assigned to write the document, which subsequently went through eleven drafts (the final draft is also printed in appendix 2).

Discussions among the group by conference call were frank and constructive. Should we be candid or diplomatic? Opinions varied, but in the end we were polite, nonconfrontational, and informational. In the words of the title we chose, we aimed to find "common ground." Thinking the mission hopeless or that a hostile administration would use us to greenwash generally awful policies, several members dropped out along the way. The rest of us proceeded in good faith fully aware of that possibility.

As a teacher, I regarded the effort as a form of remedial education.

After 9/11, the context changed dramatically. In light of that event we rewrote much of the paper in order to highlight connections between real security, prosperity, climate stability, environmental protection, and fairness. These, we argued, were not separate issues, but different facets of one big issue: the conduct of the public business. Real security, in other words, requires a systems approach to national policy across a range of issues. Relative to increasing energy efficiency and using wind or solar, for example, the administration's plan to build more nuclear power plants would only create more targets for terrorists and drain the economy of investment capital. In short, we aimed to establish the relationship between farsighted national policy and a practical environmental movement that included prominent corporations. We believed that such an approach would be in the national interest and possibly set U.S. politics on a new course.

Perhaps naively, all of us regarded the effort as a public duty. What we had to say was contrary to the emerging policies of the administration, but not to logic, fact, or even to the administration's political advantage. Indeed, America's great leaders have always emerged from epoch-defining events, as the terrorist attacks on 9/11 seemed so clearly to be. And when they rose to meet the challenges of their time, great presidents such as Lincoln and Roosevelt called the American people to higher levels of patriotism, sacrifice, and nobility, not to fear and pettiness. In doing so they placed the trials and tribulations of war into larger contexts that redefined us as a free and democratic people in changing circumstances. Similarly, we proposed that the terrorist attacks of 9/11 be seen against the realities of the twenty-first century. The paper, accordingly, began with words from a Central Intelligence Agency report:

It is time to understand "the environment" for what it is: the national-security issue of the early 21st century. The political and strategic impact of surging populations, spreading disease, deforestation and soil erosion, water depletion, air pollution, and possibly rising sea levels in critical, overcrowded regions . . . will prompt mass migrations and, in turn, incite group conflicts that will be the core foreign-policy challenge from which most others will ultimately emanate, arousing the public and uniting assorted interests left over from the Cold War.

These environmental concerns are related to the larger human agenda. For, "Whatever else divides humankind, we share a common dependence on the waters, air, soils, and life systems of the Earth. These are given to us as a sacred trust to be passed on to all those who will follow."

We intended to say nothing partisan or ideological. Rather, we appealed to the need to heal divisions of politics, region, class, and generation, saying that the administration had a great opportunity to "build sustainable prosperity in ways that increase our security, remain true to our national heritage, and serve the best traditions of both political parties [and] a rare opportunity in which the right things to do from a long-term perspective, properly done, can also increase near-term advantages."

To resolve problems of environment, economy, and equity we proposed five principles deliberately stated in the accommodating language of business:

1. Well-run businesses seek to build capital. By the same logic building the natural capital of soils, forests, and ecosystem services that sustain life, health, and prosperity is essential to our well-being.
2. Like a well-run business, the economy should operate on income not principal; i.e. we would do well to speed the transition to the next economy based on resource efficiency and renewable energy.
3. Recent advances in materials science, advanced technology, and systems design, many of which mimic natural processes, should be at the forefront of national innovation.
4. Accepted principles of accounting include the gains and losses of capital. By a similar logic we should account fully for the loss or increase in natural capital in our esti-

mates of national wealth. Using GDP as a measure to guide our affairs is as unreliable as asking a business to keep its accounts by adding expenses to income, instead of subtracting them.

5. Solutions lie in understanding the causes that link security, economics, ethics, health, and ecology. Accordingly, seek solutions that solve more than one problem by working across conventional boundaries.

Our specific recommendations aimed to encourage administration support for policies that increased the efficiency with which we use energy, water, and materials, reduce pollution, and protect land, soils, forests, and biotic capital while building "security by design." We proposed that the "administration make a resolute announcement that the United States will end its dependence on insecure sources of foreign oil, increase energy efficiency, and harness renewable energy sources."

The benefits? By doing so we could remove ourselves from the politics of an unstable region, lower our balance of payments deficit, reduce air pollution, support domestic industries, create many new jobs, establish the foundations for a solar-hydrogen economy, lower the emission of greenhouse gases, and reduce our vulnerability to terrorists and technological failures.

The document concluded by placing environment, energy, and security issues within a larger historical framework:

Three times in American history a generation of patriots rose to do its duty with greatness. The generation of the American Revolution threw off tyranny and created a nation based on the belief that all humans are created equal. The generation of the U.S. Civil War, rose to its Great Work by giving those words meaning by ending slavery. The generation now passing faced down the perils of Fascism and Communism while building the basis for American prosperity. The challenges of our time are at least as daunting as any before and will demand no less courage, vision, spiritual depth, and statesmanship. We, like those before us, will be judged not by short-term political success, but by whether we rise to do our Great Work. The challenges of our time are like no other. They are both global and local. They include both eliminating terrorism and eliminating pollution described in "parts per billion" and measured over decades or centuries. They are complex, and lie at the intersection of human behavior and natural systems. Hardest of all, they are mostly caused by past successes, not failures. To rise to our challenges and do our work greatly will require extraordinary clarity of mind and the courage to do what is right in the long term. It will require the creativity to adapt institutions and habits born in an agrarian world to a largely urban world of six, soon to be eight billion people and more. Above all, it will require a change in how we see ourselves relative to other life forms and to future generations. These are the standards by which our great grandchildren will judge us. No generation has ever had greater work to do, and none had more reason to rise to greatness.

On October 11 four of us, representing the larger group, went to the White House: Ray Anderson, president and founder of Interface Inc.; Bo Callaway, former secretary of the army under the first President Bush; Hunter Lovins, cofounder of the Rocky Mountain Institute; and me. Before leaving our hotel we reviewed our "game plan," rather like Don Quixote and Sancho Panza reviewing the state of their equipment prior to charging a windmill. Bo was our chief spokesperson, but we were all to chime in as appropriate; in other words we would play it by ear.

The day was a beautiful, clear fall day in Washington, but the air of siege was evident. The previous day witnessed the first bioterrorism alert and the tension throughout the city was high. We walked around concrete barricades, past numerous police, and through security clearance into the executive office building. By coincidence, Ralph Reed, founder of the Christian Coalition and sometime Enron consultant, walked toward us with the full confidence of a man who knows his way around the place. He and Bo greeted each other warmly and we went on to the appointed room, a large ornate space with a high ceiling and a long conference table.

When the meeting commenced it did so without the principals from the administration. Mr. Rove was detained but was said to be on his way. The vice president, the secretary of the interior, and the head of the EPA were meeting with the president. The meeting had a large number of young White House staffers, but the chief spokesperson was a lawyer, James Connaughton, now working as the head of the president's Council on Environmental Quality, which has become a vestigial enterprise. He was energetic, confident, and unmovable.

The conversation was lengthy, polite, and oblique to the real issues. We were supplicants asking for reasonableness from people working for unreasonable masters. Bo explained that our enterprise arose out of concern among moderate Republicans about the administration's hostility to the environment. To establish the possibility that we were not extremists, he cited the Republican Party tradition from Teddy Roosevelt through Richard Nixon to George H. W. Bush, a descending line. Eyes began to glaze. At some point the document we had laboriously drafted was pushed across the table and pointedly ignored. (We had decided not to send copies prior to the meeting on the assumption that doing so would have provided a reason to cancel the meeting before we had had a hearing.)

Our title, *Common Ground/Common Future,* must have appeared presumptive, perhaps even humorous, to the politely gathered, none of whom seemed aware that the administration needed to look for common ground. Nor did they seem to be thinking about any future, common or otherwise, beyond the next election.

Ray, a successful, conscientious, and imaginative capitalist, pointed out that Interface Inc., a leading manufacturer of carpet tile, was surviving in an economic downturn because of major investments the company made in energy efficiency and renewable energy. Still, not so much as a twitch of interest or even mild curiosity. Poker faces all around. Hunter attempted to place environmental and energy issues on a firm policy ground by citing the CIA study mentioned above to the effect that the environment would be the defining issue of the twenty-first century. That, too, aroused no particular response or surprise. We talked at length about the ways in which issues are linked and that effective solutions required understanding those linkages. We talked about the convergence of ethics and self-interest, a rare thing in public policy. They agreed to take the results of the conversation and copies of *Common Ground/Common Future* to their superiors who were unable to attend. There was some talk about other meetings, which subsequently did not happen. After nearly two hours we went our way and they theirs.

It was late afternoon when we walked out into the sunshine. Personally, I felt relieved. Nothing said during the meeting suggested that we'd gained any ground or sparked any real interest among the White House staff present. The body language, comments, and tone were noncommittal, suggesting politeness but not interest or curiosity.

Upshot

There was none. The morning after the meeting I had breakfast with a veteran White House lawyer who had worked for Presidents Reagan, Bush, Clinton, and now the current incumbent. She described this as the most closed administration anyone could recall, and that is saying a great deal. These were good old boys, mostly from Texas or at least with oil and coal connections, fortified by a zealous version of Christianity and hyped-up nationalism magnified by the exigencies of terrorism. And they smelled opportunity.

If our document was read, we were never told. There were to be other meetings, but they were never scheduled. The most tangible result was a Christmas card I received more than a year later from George and Laura Bush in December of 2002 with the inscription, "For the Lord is Good; his mercy is everlasting; and his truth endureth to all generations," followed by, "May love and peace fill your heart and home during this holiday season and throughout the new year. 2002." The president's signature was illegible, but this was a busy time for him, given Christmas and planning for the war against Iraq and all. The First Lady's signature was entirely legible, befitting a good librarian.

Nearly a year an a half later I was asked to participate in another meeting with White House staff to draft some ill-defined environmental agenda. I thought it over for a day or two but declined in an e-mail, saying,

> I've spent the last several days mulling over our efforts and particularly my role in this endeavor. First, I greatly appreciate your role in trying to engage the White House in a positive dialogue to improve the national environmental and energy policies. But I write to say that I do not wish to work on insignificant changes at the margins of the problem. The administration continues to advance a badly flawed energy policy that seems frankly aimed to reward the oil, gas, and coal industries. If ever there was a time to reconsider that policy, it is now in the midst of a national emergency caused largely by our persistent refusal to come to grips with our dependence on fossil fuels. The facts have been known for a long time, and are adequately summarized in the document that we presented on October 11, 2001. Improving energy efficiency and phasing in renewables is cheaper by orders of magnitude than increasing supply and offers collateral benefits for the environment and the economy while protecting the interests of our grandchildren. None of this is new information. The administration is using the events of

September 11th, cynically I think, to push through an energy bill that should never have seen the light of day. If I am wrong and they are ready to acknowledge the need for our help and perspective I will gladly admit my error and do all that I can to help them change course. But lacking such evidence I believe that my time would be better spent on other things.

Sincerely,
David W. Orr

Our group hoped to find an opening to convey the news that this is one world, things are connected often in ironic ways, what goes around comes around, violence in all of its forms is self-defeating, and that the long term isn't all that far off. The news was delivered, but no one was home.

Common Ground/Common Future

Preamble. We represent a group of U.S. citizens with varying backgrounds in business, law, government service, public organizations, research, and higher education.[1] The group comes from a diversity of regions, religious perspectives, and political opinions, but is joined in the belief that the security of the nation, the health of our economy, and our common future depend on the wise management of our common natural environment. The stewardship of the world to be inherited by our children and theirs must transcend party and short-term interests. Whatever else divides humankind, we share a common dependence on the waters, air, soils, and life systems of the Earth. These are given to us as a sacred trust to be passed on to all those who will follow.

Ours is a time of both danger and opportunity. Effective and farsighted stewardship will make the difference between very different human futures. On one hand, better design and improved technology make it possible to increase resource efficiency, and decrease pollution radically, to establish sustainable prosperity, and to improve equity within and between generations for all the world's people. Failure to take full advantage of possibilities now before us will commit us to a darker future of increased political turmoil, terrorism, pollution, conflict over resources, adverse climatic change, and suffering. The time to make decisive changes is perilously short.

We have been asked by Mr. Karl Rove through the good offices of Mr. Bo Callaway to suggest practical ways in which environmental preservation and restoration can increase security and economic prosperity. We offer a new and exciting body of knowledge about how to solve diverse problems simultaneously and sustainably. We draw on our collective experience, the sciences, and, not the least, the Republican Party's tradition of concern for the environment that has been the hallmark of administrations from the presidency of Theodore Roosevelt through that of George H. W. Bush. We appreciate the opportunity to meet with representatives of President George W. Bush, and offer this document that derives from our common interest in creating a secure, sustainable, prosperous, and just future for all people.

Unifying Principles

National security, energy policy, climate, the environment, and economic development are linked in ways that few have acknowledged. In the aftermath of the recent terrorist attacks, many analysts and citizens are realizing that America's energy supply is vulnerable. Not only do we import more than half the oil we use, but many of our domestic supply technologies can be attacked in ways that would be devastating to our ability to supply energy and dangerous to surrounding populations. It is tempting to say that any domestic source is more secure than any foreign one, but this is simply not true. As was demonstrated in "Energy Policies for Resilience and National Security," a 1981 report for the Pentagon, many major oil and gas lines, electric grids, and power stations can be quickly cut off.[3] That vulnerability has if anything increased in the 20 years since, and current national energy policy would inadvertently increase it further.

Ensuring the security of American supplies will require an energy system that is resilient by design. New technologies now on the market, combined with more efficient use of energy, can achieve this at lower cost than the systems now in place or proposed. Implementing such a system of distributed generation will create more jobs than conventional energy supplies, will greatly reduce the threat to the climate, and will reduce many other environmental harms. This was demonstrated over the last 10 years by the Sacramento Municipal Utility District. Forced to shut its poorly performing nuclear reactor, it was able to replace the power rapidly and economically with a diverse mix of small-scale, distributed supply technologies and energy efficiency. Not only is the utility better off financially than it would have been had it continued to operate the reactor, but the surrounding community is as well.

For many reasons, environmental issues have become contentious, dividing region against region, party against party, faction against faction, and, if not resolved, the present generation against the legitimate interests of its descendents. Such divisions are costly, counterproductive, and unnecessary. Below is evidence from a growing body of corporate experience, local, state, and federal initiatives that there are good ways to resolve most, if not all, environmental problems in ways that enhance global security and prosperity while honoring our childrenís future. Finding common ground requires transcending false divisions between:

- Short-term interests and long-term necessity,
- Economics and ecology, and
- Left and right.

Doing so would help to heal the wounds inflicted by political contention, competing ideologies, and misinformation. Our single message is that America can build sustainable prosperity in ways that increase our security, remain true to our national heritage, and serve the best traditions of both political parties. We have a rare opportunity in which the right things to do from a long-term perspective, properly done, can also increase near-term advantages. Evidence from public polls consistently shows that the American people overwhelmingly regard environmental protection as an issue that ought to transcend party affiliation. In the appendices we offer detailed case studies that demonstrate how new technologies and design approaches can profitably reduce or eliminate pollution and depletion in many ways. Consider these indicative examples:[4]

- DuPont recently announced that by 2010, it will reduce its carbon dioxide (CO_2) emissions by 65% from 1990 levels, raise its revenues 6% a year with no increase in energy use, and get a tenth of its energy and a quarter of its raw materials from renewables, all in the name of increasing shareholder value. By 1999 it had reduced greenhouse gas emissions 49%, held worldwide energy use flat, and increased production 35%.

- STMicroelectronics, the world's sixth-largest semi-conductor chipmaker, has set a goal of zero net carbon emissions by 2010 despite a 40-fold increase in production from 1990, in pursuit of commercial advantage. By 2000, they had already achieved 29% reduction in electricity consumption, 45% drop in water usage, and 29% decrease in the emission of greenhouse gasses. The radical efficiency gains that can cut their carbon emissions per chip by 92% profitably now and 98–99% profitably soon also make their factories work better and make new ones faster.

- Interface Inc., a global commercial interiors company, sought to increase the productivity with which they use energy and materials by systematically identifying and eliminating waste in their worldwide operations. From 1994 to mid-2001, this added $167 million to the bottom line, and now provides 27% of the company's operating profit. In 1997–98, Interface doubled revenues, tripled operating profits, and nearly doubled employment. Its latest quarter-billion dollars of revenue have been produced with no increase in energy or materials inputs, just from mining internal waste, closing resource loops, eliminating toxics, and shifting toward a service model.

- Southwire Corporation, the biggest independent maker of cable, rod and wire, halved its energy per pound of product in six years. The savings roughly equaled the company's profits during a period when many competitors were going bankrupt. This energy efficiency effort probably saved 4,000 jobs at 10 plants in six states.

- Dow Chemical's 2,400-worker Louisiana Division implemented more than 900 worker-suggested energy-saving projects during 1981–93, with average annual returns on investment in excess of 200%. Both returns and savings tended to rise in the latter years, even after the annual savings had passed $100 million, because the engineers were learning new ways to save faster than they were using up the old ones.

The United States has already cut its annual energy bill by $200 billion since the first oil shock in 1973, but still wastes $300 billion worth of energy each year. Just the energy thrown away by U.S. power stations as waste heat equals the total energy used by Japan for everything. Over the past quarter century, reduced energy intensity has become the nation's largest energy supply. It's over 5 times as big as domestic oil output in this country, over twice oil imports, over 12 times Persian Gulf oil imports, and the fastest-growing source, and it's mostly because of technical efficiency. In fact, we've doubled our oil productivity in the past quarter century, yet barely scratched the surface of the efficiency that's available and worth buying.

In short, the efficiency with which we use energy, water, and materials can be dramatically increased, waste and pollution reduced, and land, soils, forests, and biotic capital enhanced without the burdens of excessive government intervention. Such measures not only improve bottom-line performance but increase the security of companies and the country. For example, energy efficiency cannot be cut off. The growing contribution to the nation's energy supply from energy produced in such smaller, distributed forms of generation as gas-fired co-generation and the various forms of renewables is similarly immune to terrorist attack. Wind power around the world is now adding more gigawatts of supply each year than nuclear power did each year during the 1990s. Wind power is growing 24% each year and costs about the same as just running a coal or nuclear plant (thus much cheaper than a new plant).[5]

Water supply and demand will be a source of regional conflicts in years ahead. A recent CIA report warned that:

> The outlook for water is troubling. By 2015 nearly half the world's population—more than 3 billion people—will live in countries that are "water-stressed"—having less than 1,700 cubic meters of water per capita per year—mostly in Africa, the Middle East, South Asia, and northern China. [6]

But just as with energy, well-designed resource-savings programs can dramatically and profitably solve these problems to everyone's advantage.

- Staff of the Grand Wailea Hotel & Resort conducted an eco-audit and developed retrofit strategies for the largest resort on Maui. Implementing recommendations from Rocky Mountain Institute, they were able, in a one-week trial, to cut water use by 48% and associated energy use by similar amounts, for potential resource savings worth more than $1 million annually, all without diminishing the guest experience.
- The University of California at Santa Barbara implemented a comprehensive water-efficiency program that reduced total campus water use by nearly 50%, even as the campus population increased. This saved $3.7 million over a seven-year period, excluding energy and maintenance savings.
- In the mainly African American and Hispanic neighborhoods of East Los Angeles, CTSI Corporation partnered with Mothers of East LA to distribute water and energy efficient devices. People brought their inefficient old toilets to exchange for new ones plus high-performance showerheads and compact fluorescent lamps. This swap cut water and energy bills

by about $30–120 per household per year, putting money back into residents' pockets and into community economies. The Metropolitan Water District of Southern California contracted with CTSI to make the program available throughout Los Angeles and Southern California. MELA-SI and eight other community groups that later joined the program earned over $1 million by participating. By the beginning of 1996, community groups working with CTSI had distributed more than 300,000 toilets, saving over 3 billion gallons of water per year and creating over a hundred jobs.

- In the 1980s, California industry cut its water intensity by 46%. Nationwide during 1980–95, water withdrawn per dollar of real GDP fell by 38%, and per person by 21%. U.S. water withdrawals have been falling for the past two decades despite growing population and GDP. Yet the water productivity revolution has only just begun.

These and other cases described in the appendices illustrate the application of five principles of solutions that resolve problems of environment, economy, and equity. We believe that they are fundamental to security and prosperity:

- Well-run businesses seek to build capital. By the same logic building the natural capital of soils, forests, and ecosystem services that sustain life, health, and prosperity is essential to our well-being.
- Like a well-run business, the economy should operate on income not principal; i.e., we would do well to speed the transition to the next economy based on resource efficiency and renewable energy.
- Recent advances in materials science, advanced technology, and systems design, many of which mimic natural processes, should be at the forefront of national innovation.
- Accepted principles of accounting include the gains and losses of capital. By a similar logic we should

account fully for the loss or increase in natural capital in our estimates of national wealth. Using GDP as a measure to guide our affairs is as unreliable as asking a business to keep its accounts by adding expenses to income, instead of subtracting them.

- Solutions lie in understanding the causes that link security, economics, ethics, health, and ecology. Accordingly, seek solutions that solve more than one problem by working across conventional boundaries.

Applying these principles to future resource decisions, as they have been in the case studies described below, will enable this administration to promote enduring American prosperity by ensuring the integrity of natural systems.

Recommendations

There are many actions to protect the environment that make good sense, and would enhance the performance of our economy. The greatest leverage, however, is to be found in the clear and empirically demonstrated linkages between issues of security, economic development, environment, and climate policy. As demonstrated in this document, these are tightly interrelated not separable policy areas. We recommend that the administration take steps to reconsider the architecture of the national energy system in light of the terrorist attacks of September 11th. Energy policy is a key component in national security, as well as in its economic planning and environmental policy.

We propose that this administration make a resolute announcement that the United States will end its dependence on insecure sources of foreign oil, increase energy efficiency, and harness renewable energy sources. Doing this would not only enable the nation to engage in the politics of an unstable region by choice, not permanent necessity, it would also lower our balance of payments deficit, reduce air pollution, support domestic industries, and create many new jobs. It would establish the technological basis for a solar-hydrogen economy, reduce the emission of greenhouse gases, and dramatically reduce our vulnerability to terrorists, as well as to acts of God.

As a first step in this process, we propose that the White House organize a conference to discuss how such a plan might be developed and implemented rationally, rapidly, and in ways that provide immediate economic advantages. Finally, we propose that this effort be conceived as a way to unify the nation, drawing together Democrats and Republicans, business and the public, and the academy and faith communities.

Conclusion

No generation ever has the luxury of choosing its particular challenges and dangers, its "Great Work." Three times in American history a generation of patriots rose to do its duty with greatness. The generation of the American Revolution threw off tyranny and created a nation based on the belief that all humans are created equal. The generation of the U.S. Civil War, rose to its Great Work by giving those words meaning by ending slavery. The generation now passing faced down the perils of fascism and communism while building the basis for American prosperity. The challenges of our time are at least as daunting as any before and will demand no less courage, vision, spiritual depth, and statesmanship. We, like those before us, will be judged not by short-term political success, but by whether we rise to do our Great Work. The challenges of our time are like no other. They are both global and local. They include both eliminating terrorism and eliminating pollution described in "parts per billion" and measured over decades or centuries. They are complex, and lie at the intersection of human behavior and natural systems. Hardest of all, they are mostly caused by past successes, not failures. To rise to our challenges and do our work greatly will require extraordinary clarity of mind and the courage to do what is right in the long-term. It will require the creativity to adapt institutions and habits born in an agrarian world to a largely urban world of six, soon to be eight billion people and more. Above all, it will require a change in how we see ourselves relative to other life forms and to future generations. These are the standards by which our great grandchildren will judge us. No generation has ever had greater work to do, and none had more reason to rise to greatness.

Introduction to the 2005 Edition

1. Thomas Berry, *The Great Work* (New York: Bell Tower, 1999).

2. David Barstow, William Broad, and Jeff Gerth, "Skewed Intelligence Data in March to War in Iraq," *New York Times,* October 3, 2004, 1, 16–18.

3. Ron Suskind, *The Price of Loyalty* (New York: Simon and Schuster, 2004), 73–86; Russ Baker, "Two Years Before 9/11, Candidate Bush Was Already Talking Privately About Attacking Iraq, According to His Former Ghost Writer" Common Dreams News Center, October 28, 2004, http://www.commondreams.org/headlines04/1028-01.htm; and Walter Pincus, "British Intelligence Warned of Iraq War" *The Washington Post* May 2005.

4. Elizabeth Drew, "Pinning the Blame," *New York Review of Books,* September 23, 2004, 6–12; and Benjamin DeMott, "Whitewash as Public Service," *Harper's Magazine,* October 2004, 35–45.

5. Karen Greenberg and Joshua Dratel, eds., *The Torture Papers: The Road to Abu Ghraib* (New York: Cambridge University Press, 2005).

6. Robert F. Kennedy, *Crimes Against Nature* (New York: Harper-Collins, 2004).

7. Joel Brinkley, "Out of Spotlight, Bush Overhauls U.S. Regulations," *New York Times,* August 14, 2004, 1, A10.

8. Eric Alterman, *What Liberal Media?* (New York: Basic Books, 2003).

9. Steven Freeman, "The Unexplained Exit Poll Discrepancy" (Working Paper no. 04-10, University of Pennsylvania, School of Arts and Sciences, Graduate Division, Center for Organizational Dynamics, November 21, 2004); and Jonathan Simon and Ron Baiman, "The 2004 Presidential Election," unpublished paper, December 28, 2004.

10. Quoted in Bob Woodward, *Bush at War* (New York: Simon and Schuster, 2003).

11. Amory Lovins et al., *Winning the Oil Endgame* (Old Snowmass, CO: Rocky Mountain Institute, 2004); and Vaclav Smil, *Energy at the Crossroads* (Cambridge, MA: MIT Press, 2003).

Chapter 1: James Madison's Nightmare

1. Richard Matthews, *If Men Were Angels* (Lawrence: University of Kansas Press, 1995), 8, 27. The title of this chapter was influenced by Matthews.

2. Lewis Lapham, "Tentacles of Rage," *Harper's Magazine*, September 2004, 31–41; and David Brock, *The Republican Noise Machine* (New York: Crown, 2004).

3. Nace, Ted, *Gangs of America: The Rise of Corporate Power and the Disabling of Democracy* (San Francisco: Berrett-Koehler, 2003), 142.

4. Brock, *Republican Noise Machine*, 74.

5. Mark Danner, "How Bush Really Won," *New York Review of Books*, January 13, 2005, 51.

6. National Endowment for the Arts (NEA), *Reading at Risk*, Research Division Report no. 46 (Washington, DC: NEA, 2004.)

7. Michael Klare, *Blood and Oil* (New York: Metropolitan Books, 2004).

8. Richard Kerr, "Climate Modelers See Scorching Future as a Real Possibility," *Science* 307 (January 28, 2005): 497; and Steve Connor, "Global Warming is 'Twice as Bad as Previously Thought,'" *Independent* (UK), January 27, 2005.

9. Deborah Tannen, "Let Them Eat Words," *American Prospect*, September 2003, 29–31; and Jennifer Lee, "A Call for Softer, Greener Language," *New York Times*, March 2, 2003.

10. Leonard Levy, *Origins of the Bill of Rights* (New Haven: Yale University Press, 1999), 85–86.

11. Forrest Church, ed., *The Separation of Church and State* (Boston: Beacon, 2004).

12. Glenn Scherer, "The Godly Must Be Crazy," *Grist Magazine*, October 27, 2004, http://www.grist.org/news/maindish/2004/10/27/scherer-christian.

13. Ben Bagdikian, *The Media Monopoly*, 6th ed. (Boston: Beacon, 2000).

14. Steven Hill, *Fixing Elections: The Failure of America's Winner Take All Politics* (London: Routledge, 2002).

15. Cass Sunstein, *The Second Bill of Rights* (New York: Basic Books, 2004).

16. Sheldon Wolin, *Politics and Vision* (Princeton: Princeton University Press, 2004), 597.

Chapter 2: Authentic Christianity and the Problem of Earthly Power

1. Linda Lear, *Rachel Carson: Witness for Nature* (New York: Henry Holt, 1997), 15.

2. Bill Moyers, "Welcome to Doomsday," *New York Review,* March 24, 2005, 8–10.

3. Bruce Bawer, *Stealing Jesus* (New York: Three Rivers Press, 1997), 83–88.

4. Louis Menand, "Permanent Fatal Errors," *New Yorker,* December 6, 2004, 54–60.

5. Jim Wallis, *God's Politics* (New York: Harper, 2005); Laurie Goodstein, "Evangelical Leaders Swing Influence Behind Effort to Combat Global Warming," *New York Times,* March 10, 2005; and Laurie Goodstein, "Evangelicals Open Debate on Widening Policy Questions," *New York Times,* March 11, 2005.

6. Elizabeth Rosenthal, "Study Puts Iraqi Deaths of Civilians at 100,000," *New York Times,* October 29, 2004.

7. Alterman, *What Liberal Media?*

8. Chalmers Johnson, *The Sorrows of Empire* (New York: Metropolitan Books, 2004).

9. Terry Kirby, "Global Warming Kills 150,000 a Year, Warns UN," *Independent* (UK), December 12, 2003.

10. Kennedy, *Crimes Against Nature.*

11. Fox Butterfield, "Record 6.9 million People in Criminal System," *San Francisco Chronicle,* July 26, 2004.

12. Pam Belluck, "To Avoid Divorce, Move to Massachusetts," *New York Times,* November 14, 2004.

13. William Stringfellow, *An Ethic for Christians and Other Aliens in a Strange Land* (Waco, TX: Word Books, 1973), 125.

Chapter 3: Walking North on a Southbound Train

1. A similar conundrum is represented by this chapter's title, which comes from Peter Montague, *Environment and Health Weekly,* no. 570 (October 30, 1997).

2. Thomas Walkom, "Return of the Old, Cold War," *Toronto Star,* September 28, 2002, F-4.

3. Anatol Lieven, "The Push for War," *London Review of Books,* October 3, 2002.

4. Jimmy Carter, "The Troubling New Face of America," *Washington Post,* September 5, 2002.

5. Jeff Gates, "Globalization's Challenge," *Reflections* 3, no. 4 (Summer 2002): 4.

6. Quoted in Curt Meine, *Conservation and the Progressive Movement* (unpublished manuscript, 2002), 4.

7. Sharon Buccino et al., *Hostile Environment: How Activist Judges Threaten Our Air, Water, and Land* (Washington, DC: Natural Resources Defense Council, 2001).

8. Jack Turner, *The Abstract Wild* (Tucson: University of Arizona Press, 1996), 21, 25.

9. Ibid., 21–22.

10. Marjorie Kelly, *The Divine Right of Capital* (San Francisco: Barrett-Koehler, 2001).

11. Vaclav Havel, "A Farewell to Politics," *The New York Review of Books,* October 24, 2002, 4.

Chapter 4: Rewriting the Ten Commandments

1. Walter Prescott Webb, *The Great Frontier* (Austin: University of Texas Press, 1951/1975), 14.

2. Ibid., 301.

3. Robert Heilbroner, *An Inquiry into the Human Prospect,* rev. ed. (New York: Norton, 1980), 175.

4. William Ophuls and Stephen Boyan, *Ecology and the Politics of Scarcity Revisited* (New York: W. H. Freeman, 1992), 315, 216.

5. Thomas Berry, *The Great Work* (New York: Bell Tower, 1999), 3.

6. Vaclav Havel, *Summer Meditations* (New York: Knopf, 1992), 6.

7. Ibid., 116.

8. Ibid., 66.

9. It is widely assumed that the decision of the Supreme Court in *Santa Clara County v. Southern Pacific Railroad* in 1886 gave the rights of natural persons, such as freedom of speech, press, and due process, to corporations. By confusing natural and artificial personhood, that decision is the fountainhead of a considerable stream of judicial mischief. For a view that the Court, in fact, said no such thing, see Thom Hartmann, *Unequal Protection* (Emmaus, PA: Rodale Press, 2002), 95–119.

10. Havel, *Summer Meditations,* 8.

Chapter 5: The Events of 9/11

1. Amory Lovins et al., *Small Is Profitable* (Old Snowmass, CO: Rocky Mountain Institute, 2002).

Chapter 6: The Labors of Sisyphus

1. Bjorn Lomborg, *The Skeptical Environmentalist* (New York: Cambridge University Press, 2001).

2. Ibid., 3.

3. Ibid., 40.

4. Ibid., 331.

5. Ibid., 328, 91, 159, 210, 329–30.

6. Ibid., 351.

7. Michael Grubb, "Relying on Manna From Heaven?" *Science* 294 (November 9, 2001): 1285.

8. Ibid., 1286.

9. Ibid.

10. Thomas Lovejoy, "Biodiversity: Dismissing Scientific Process," *Scientific American*, January 2002, 69.

11. Ibid., 71.

12. Lone Frank, "Scholarly Conduct: *Skeptical Environmentalist* Labeled 'Dishonest,'" *Science* 299 (January 17, 2003): 326.

13. Lomborg, *Skeptical Environmentalist*, 9.

14. Ibid., 35.

15. Ibid., 33.

16. Kenneth Arrow et al., "Economic Growth, Carrying Capacity, and the Environment," *Science* 268 (April 28, 1995).

17. Lomborg, *Skeptical Environmentalist*, 323.

18. This is pure sleight of hand. No one can know what the costs of abating or adjusting to climatic change will be. It is a moving target with thresholds and dynamics that no statistics or economic analysis can tell us with anything approaching certainty.

19. Grubb, "Relying on Manna From Heaven?" 1286.

20. Lomborg, *Skeptical Environmentalist*, 112–13.

21. Ibid., 63.

22. Ibid., 29.

23. Ibid., 312.

24. Matt Ridley, "The Profits of Doom," *The Spectator*, February 23, 2002, 10.

25. Ross Gelbspan, *The Heat Is On* (Reading, MA: Addison-Wesley, 1998).

Chapter 7: Four Challenges of Sustainability

1. World Commission on Environment and Development (Brundtland Commission), *Our Common Future* (New York: Oxford University Press, 1987).

2. Thomas de Zengotita, "The Numbing of the American Mind," *Harper's Magazine*, April 2002.

3. Thomas Homer-Dixon, *The Ingenuity Gap* (New York: Knopf, 2000).

4. Howard T. Odum and Elisabeth C. Odum, *A Prosperous Way Down* (Boulder: University Press of Colorado, 2001), 5.

5. Ibid., 85, 8.

6. Ibid., 133.

7. Joseph Tainter, *The Collapse of Complex Societies* (Cambridge: Cambridge University Press, 1988), 194.

8. Ibid., 198.

9. Odum and Odum, *Prosperous Way Down*, 67.

10. Michael Carley and Ian Christie, *Managing Sustainable Development* (London: Earthscan, 2000).

11. Odum and Odum, *Prosperous Way Down*, 258.

12. Ibid., 262.

13. E. F. Schumacher, *A Guide for the Perplexed* (New York: Harper and Row, 1977), 120–22.

14. Ibid., 127.

15. Lynn Margulis, *The Symbiotic Planet* (London: Phoenix, 1998), 149.

16. Ernest Becker, *The Denial of Death* (New York: Free Press, 1973), 11, ix.

17. Ibid.

18. Ibid., 284.

19. Ibid.

Chapter 8: Leverage

1. Norman Vig and Michael Kraft, eds. *Environmental Policy* 4th edition. (Washington, DC: Congressional Quarterly Press, 2000).

2. Lynton Keith Caldwell, *The National Environmental Policy Act* (Bloomington: Indiana University Press, 1998).

3. Richard Andrews, *Managing the Environment, Managing Ourselves*. (New Haven: Yale University Press, 1999), 370.

4. Gretchen Daily, ed., *Nature's Services* (Washington, DC: Island Press, 1997).

5. Paul Hawken, Amory Lovins, and Hunter Lovins, *Natural Capitalism* (Boston: Little, Brown, 1999).

6. Colin Price, *Time, Discounting, and Value* (London: Routledge, 1993), 345.

7. Ibid., 345–47.

8. Donella Meadows, "Economic Laws Clash with Planets," *Earthlight*, Spring 2001.

9. Norman Myers, *Perverse Subsidies* (Washington, DC: Island Press, 2001), xvi–xvii.

10. Ibid., xviii.

11. Daniel Lazare, *America's Undeclared War* (New York: Harcourt, 2001), 223.

12. Robert Frank, *Luxury Fever* (Princeton: Princeton University Press, 1999), 267.

13. Donella Meadows, "Places to Intervene in a System," *Whole Earth*, Winter 1997, 84.

Chapter 9: A Literature of Redemption

1. See Jonathan Glover, *Humanity: A Moral History of the Twentieth Century,* (New Haven: Yale University Press, 1999).

2. W. E. B. DuBois, *Writings* (New York: The Library of America, 1986), 1046.

3. Lillian Smith, *Killers of the Dream* (New York: Norton, 1978), 228.

4. Henry Steele Commager, *Documents of American History* (New York: Appleton-Century-Crofts, 1963), 342.

5. Donald Griffin, *The Question of Animal Awareness* (New York: Rockefeller University Press, 1981), 170.

6. Donald Griffin, *Animal Minds* (Chicago: University of Chicago Press, 1992), 252–53.

7. Griffin, *Animal Awareness,* 170.

8. Roger Fouts, *Next of Kin* (New York: William Morrow, 1997), 372.

9. Ibid., 407.

10. Steven Wise, *Rattling the Cage* (Cambridge, MA: Perseus Books, 2000), 270.

Chapter 10: Diversity

1. Richard Leaky and Roger Lewin, *The Sixth Extinction* (New York: Doubleday, 1995).

2. E. O. Wilson, *The Diversity of Life* (Cambridge, MA: Harvard University Press, 1992), 342.

3. Lewis Mumford, *Technics and Civilization* (New York: Harcourt, Brace, and World, 1934), 15.

4. Ibid., 17.

5. Alfred Crosby, *The Measure of Reality* (Cambridge: Cambridge University Press, 1997), 229.

6. Stephen Toulmin, *Cosmopolis* (Chicago: University of Chicago Press, 1990), 35.

7. Stephen Toulmin, *Return to Reason* (Cambridge, MA: Harvard University Press, 2001), 78.

8. Ibid., 204.

9. Andro Linklater, *Measuring America* (New York: Walker, 2002).

10. Quoted in ibid., 73.

11. James C. Scott, *Seeing like a State* (New Haven: Yale University Press, 1998), 4.

12. Theodore Porter, *Trust in Numbers* (Princeton: Princeton University Press, 1995), 85.

13. E. O. Wilson, *The Future of Life* (New York: Knopf, 2002), 156.

14. Paul Ehrlich and E. O. Wilson, "Biodiversity Studies: Science and Policy," *Science* 253 (1991): 761.

15. Edmund Burke, the founder of modern conservatism, put it this way: "Men are qualified for civil liberty in exact proportion to their dis-

position to put moral chains upon their own appetites. . . . Society cannot exist unless a controlling power upon will and appetite be placed somewhere, and the less of it there is within, the more there must be without. It is ordained in the eternal constitution of things, that men of intemperate minds cannot be free. Their passions forge their fetters" (quoted in William Ophuls and Stephen Boyan, *Ecology and the Politics of Scarcity Revisited* [New York: W. H. Freeman, 1992]).

Chapter 11: The Uses of Prophecy

1. Jaquetta Hawkes, *A Land* (Boston: Houghton-Mifflin, 1950), 202.

2. Victor Davis Hanson, *Fields without Dreams* (New York: Free Press, 1996), 282.

3. Ibid., 274–75.

4. Ibid., xi.

5. Abraham Heschel, *The Prophets: An Introduction* (New York: Harper Torchbooks, 1969), 7.

6. Liberty Hyde Bailey, *The Holy Earth* (Ithaca: New York State College of Agriculture, 1980), 27.

7. George Orwell, *A Collection of Essays* (New York: Harcourt, Brace, Jovanovich, 1981), 157.

8. Becker, *Denial of Death*, 268.

9. Ibid., 156.

10. Ibid., 151.

11. Ibid., 153.

12. Eric Freyfogle, ed. *The New Agrarianism* (Washington, DC: Island Press, 2001), xiii.

Chapter 12: The Constitution of Nature

1. Fareed Zakaria, *The Future of Freedom* (New York: Norton, 2003).

2. Robert Dahl, *How Democratic Is the American Constitution?* (New Haven: Yale University Press, 2002).

3. Howard Mumford Jones. *The Age of Energy* (New York: Viking Press, 1971), 37; see also Michael Kammen, *A Machine That Would Go of Itself* (New York: Knopf, 1987).

4. Dahl, *How Democratic Is the American Constitution?*, 118.

5. See, for example, Heinz Center, *The State of the Nation's Ecosystems* (New York: Cambridge University Press, 2002); Robin Abell, et al., *Freshwater Ecoregions of North America: A Conservation Assessment* (Washington, DC: Island Press, 2000); Taylor Ricketts, et al., *Terrestrial Ecoregions of North America: A Conservation Assessment* (Washington, DC: Island Press, 1999); and U.S. Geological Survey, *Status and Trends of the Nation's Biological Resources*, 2 vols. (Washington, DC: U.S. Government Printing Office, 1998).

6. Richard Matthews, *If Men Were Angels* (Lawrence: University of Kansas Press, 1995), 210.

7. J. R. McNeill, *Something New Under the Sun* (New York: Norton, 2000).

8. Bruce Ledewitz, "Establishing a Federal Constitutional Right to a Healthy Environment in Us and in Our Posterity," *Mississippi Law Journal* 68, no. 2 (1998): 605.

9. Bill McKibben, *Enough* (New York: Times Books, 2003).

10. Bruno Latour, *We Have Never Been Modern,* trans. Catherine Porter (Cambridge, MA: Harvard University Press, 1993), 13–15; and Ledewitz, "The Constitutions of Sustainable Capitalism and Beyond," 233–234.

11. Latour, *Never Been Modern,* 14.

12. Ibid., 15.

13. Aldo Leopold, *A Sand County Almanac,* (New York: Oxford University Press, 1949), 204, 223.

14. Latour, *Never Been Modern,*139.

15. Jones, *Age of Energy,* 107.

16. Latour, *Never Been Modern.*

17. Leopold, *Sand County Almanac,* 203–4; see also Christopher Stone, *Should Trees Have Standing?* (Los Altos, CA: William Kaufman, 1974).

18. Joe Thornton, *Pandora's Poison* (Cambridge, MA: MIT Press, 2000).

19. E. O. Wilson, *Biophilia* (Cambridge, MA: Harvard University Press, 1984), 85.

20. Ibid., 139.

21. Steven Kelman, "Why Public Ideas Matter," in *The Power of Public Ideas,* ed. Robert Reich (Cambridge, MA: Harvard University Press, 1988), 49. Emphasis added.

22. Dahl, *How Democratic Is the American Constitution?,* 154–56.

23. Charles A. Beard, *An Economic Interpretation of the Constitution of the United States* (New York: Free Press, 1935).

24. Lynton Keith Caldwell, *The National Environmental Policy Act* (Bloomington: Indiana University Press, 1998),147.

25. Ledewitz, "Constitutional Right to a Healthy Environment," 620.

26. Ibid., 631.

27. David Bollier, *Silent Theft* (London: Routledge, 2003).

28. Augustus Cochran, *Democracy Heading South* (Lawrence: University of Kansas Press, 2001),191; see also Bollier, *Silent Theft.*

29. Carolyn Raffensperger and Joel Tickner, eds., *Protecting Public Health and the Environment* (Washington, DC: Island Press, 1999).

31. Cass Sunstein, *The Partial Constitution* (Cambridge, MA: Harvard University Press, 1993), 354.

32. Ledewitz, "Constitutional Right to a Healthy Environment," 620, 567.

Chapter 14: Postscript

1. Amory Lovins, et al., *Small Is Profitable*, (Old Snowmass, CO: Rocky Mountain Institute, 2002).

2. Ibid.

3. Jonathan Schell, *The Unconquerable World* (New York: Metropolitan Books, 2003).

4. Gary Gardner, *Invoking the Spirit*, Worldwatch Paper no. 164 (Washington, DC: Worldwatch Institute, 2002); and Mary E. Tucker, *Worldly Wonder* (Chicago: Open Court, 2003).

Appendix 2: Common Ground/Common Future

1. This paper was drafted by Dr. David Orr, Chair of the Environmental Studies Program, Oberlin College, and L. Hunter Lovins, CEO Rocky Mountain Institute. The committee that charged them with drafting this includes Ray C. Anderson, Chair of Interface Inc.; Richard C. Bartlett, Vice Chairman, Mary Kay, Inc.; Howard H. Callaway, Chairman, Callaway Gardens; Dr. Becky Champion, Director of Oxbow Meadows Environmental Center, Columbus State University; LuAnn Craighton, Director of Land Stewardship, Callaway Gardens; Walter Link, Chair, The Global Academy; Amory Lovins, Rocky Mountain Institute; Patrick Noonan, Chairman, The Conservation Fund; Deana M. Perlmutter, Senior Vice President, The Dutko Group, Inc.; Dr. Peter H. Raven, Director, Missouri Botanical Garden; Edward Skloot, Executive Director, The Surdna Foundation.

2. Jeffrey B. White, "A Different Kind of Threat: Some Thoughts on Irregular Warfare," *Studies in Intelligence* 39, no. 5 (1996), http://www.cia.gov/csi/studies/96unclass/iregular.htm.

3. L. Hunter Lovins and Armory B. Lovins, "Energy Policies for Resilience and National Security," Defense Technical Information Center accession no. A108263, 1981. The popular book *Brittle Power*, based on this work, will soon be available on the Rocky Mountain Institute Web site, http://www.rmi.org.

4. These and many other examples can be found in L. Hunter Lovins and Amory B. Lovins, "Natural Capitalism: Path to Sustainability?" Rocky Mountain Institute, 2001, http://www.rmi.org/images/other/Bus_NatCapPathToSustain.pdf.

5. Amory B. Lovins, "Why Nuclear Power's Failure in the Marketplace Is Irreversible" (Fortunately for Nonproliferation and Climate Protection)" (speech to the Nuclear Control Institute, Washington, D.C., April 9, 2001), http://www.nci.org/.

6. John C. Gannon, Chairman, National Intelligence Council, "The Role of Intelligence Services In a Globalized World" (remarks at the Conference Sponsored by Friedrich Ebert Stiftung, Berlin, Germany, May 21, 2001), http://www.cia.gov/nic/speeches/speeches/role_intel_services.htm.

Abell, Robin, David Olson, Eric Dinerstein, and Patrick
    Hurley. *Freshwater Ecoregions of North America: A Conservation
    Assessment*. Washington, DC: Island Press, 2000.
Allen, Robert. *How to Save the World: Strategy for World Conservation*.
    Totowa, NJ: Barnes and Noble, 1980.
Alterman, Eric. *What Liberal Media?* New York: Basic Books, 2003.
Andrews, Richard. *Managing the Environment, Managing
    Ourselves*. New Haven: Yale University Press, 1999.
Arrow, Kenneth, et al. "Economic Growth, Carrying Capacity, and the
    Environment." *Science* 268 (April 28, 1995): 520–21.
Bagdikian, Ben. *The Media Monopoly*. 6th ed. Boston: Beacon, 2000.
Bailey, Liberty Hyde. *The Holy Earth*. Ithaca: New York State
    College of Agriculture, 1980.
Baker, Russ. "Two Years Before 9/11, Candidate Bush Was Already Talk-
    ing Privately About Attacking Iraq, According to His Former Ghost

Writer." Common Dreams News Center, October 29, 2004.
http://www.commondreams.org/headlines04/1028-01.htm.

Barstow, David, William Broad, and Jeff Gerth. "Skewed Intelligence Data in March to War in Iraq." *New York Times,* October 3, 2004.

Bawer, Bruce. *Stealing Jesus.* New York: Three Rivers Press, 1997.

Beard, Charles A. *An Economic Interpretation of the Constitution of the United States.* New York: Free Press, 1935.

Becker, Ernest. *The Denial of Death.* New York: Free Press, 1973

———. *Escape from Evil.* New York: Free Press, 1975.

Belluck, Pam. "To Avoid Divorce, Move to Massachusetts." *New York Times,* November 14, 2004.

Berry, Thomas. *The Great Work.* New York: Bell Tower, 1999.

Berry, Wendell. *Unsettling of America.* San Francisco: Sierra Club Books, 1977.

———. *Life Is a Miracle.* New York: Counterpoint, 2000.

Bollier, David. *Silent Theft.* London: Routledge, 2002.

Brinkley, Joel. "Out of Spotlight, Bush Overhauls U.S. Regulations." *New York Times,* August 14, 2004.

Brock, David. *The Republican Noise Machine.* New York: Crown, 2004.

Brown, Lester. *Building a Sustainable Society.* New York: Norton, 1980.

Buccino, S., et al. *Hostile Environment: How Activist Judges Threaten Our Air, Water, and Land.* Washington, DC: Natural Resources Defense Council, 2001.

Butterfield, Fox. "Record 6.9 million People in Criminal System." *San Francisco Chronicle,* July 26, 2004.

Caldwell, Lynton Keith. *The National Environmental Policy Act.* Bloomington: Indiana University Press, 1998.

Carley, Michael, and Ian Christie. *Managing Sustainable Development.* London: Earthscan, 2000.

Carter, Jimmy "The Troubling New Face of America." *Washington Post,* September 5, 2002.

Church, Forrest, ed. *The Separation of Church and State.* Boston: Beacon, 2004.

Cochran, Augustus. *Democracy Heading South.* Lawrence: University of Kansas Press, 2001.

Commager, Henry Steele. *Documents of American History.* New York: Appleton-Century-Crofts, 1963.

Connor, Steve. "Global Warming is 'Twice as Bad as Previously Thought.'" *Independent* (UK), January 27, 2005.

Crosby, Alfred. *The Measure of Reality.* Cambridge: Cambridge University Press, 1997.

Dahl, Robert. *How Democratic Is the American Constitution?* New Haven: Yale University Press, 2002.

Daily, Gretchen, ed. *Nature's Services.* Washington, DC: Island Press, 1997.

Danner, Mark. "How Bush Really Won." *New York Review of Books*, January 13, 2005, 48–53.

DeMott, Benjamin. "Whitewash as Public Service." *Harper's Magazine*, October 2004, 35–45.

de Zengotita, Thomas. "The Numbing of the American Mind." *Harper's Magazine*, April 2002, 33–40.

Doctorow, E. L. "In the Eighth Circle of Thieves." *The Nation*, August 7/14, 2000, 13–18.

Drew, Elizabeth. "Pinning the Blame." *New York Review of Books*, September 23, 2004, 6–12.

DuBois, W. E. B. *Writings*. New York: The Library of America, 1986.

Ehrlich, Paul, and E. O. Wilson. "Biodiversity Studies: Science and Policy." *Science* 253 (August 1991): 758–62.

Fouts, Roger. *Next of Kin*. New York: William Morrow, 1997.

Freyfogle, Eric, ed. *The New Agrarianism*. Washington, DC: Island Press, 2001.

———. *The Land We Share*. Washington, DC: Island Press, 2003.

Frank, Robert. *Luxury Fever*. Princeton: Princeton University Press, 1999.

Freeman, Steven. "The Unexplained Exit Poll Discrepancy." Working Paper #04-10, University of Pennsylvania, School of Arts and Sciences, Graduate Division, Center for Organizational Dynamics, November 21, 2004.

Gardner, Gary. *Invoking the Spirit*. Worldwatch Paper no. 164. Washington, DC: Worldwatch Institute, 2002.

Gates, Jeff. "Globalization's Challenge." *Reflections* 3, no. 4 (Summer 2002).

Gelbspan, Ross. *The Heat is On*. Reading, MA: Addison-Wesley, 1998.

Glover, Jonathan. *Humanity: A Moral History of the Twentieth Century*. New Haven: Yale University Press, 1999.

Goodall, Jane. *Reasons for Hope*. New York: Time Warner, 1999.

Goodstein, Laurie. "Evangelical Leaders Swing Influence Behind Effort to Combat Global Warming." *New York Times*, March 10, 2005.

———. "Evangelicals Open Debate on Widening Policy Questions." *New York Times*, March 11, 2005.

Greenberg, Karen, and Joshua Dratel, eds. *The Torture Papers: The Road to Abu Ghraib*. New York: Cambridge University Press, 2005.

Griffin, Donald. *Animal Minds*. Chicago: University of Chicago Press, 1992.

———. *The Question of Animal Awareness*. New York: Rockefeller University Press, 1981.

Grubb, Michael. "Relying on Manna From Heaven?" *Science* 294 (November 9, 2001): 1285–86.

Hanson, Victor Davis. *Fields without Dreams*. New York: Free Press, 1996.

Hartmann, Thom. *Unequal Protection*. Emmaus, PA: Rodale Press, 2002.

Havel, Vaclav. "A Farewell to Politics." *The New York Review of Books,* October 24, 2002.

———. *Summer Meditations.* New York: Knopf, 1992.

Hawken, Paul, Amory Lovins, and Hunter Lovins. *Natural Capitalism.* Boston: Little, Brown, 1999.

Hawkes, Jacquetta. *A Land.* Boston: Houghton-Mifflin, 1950.

Heilbroner, Robert. *An Inquiry into the Human Prospect.* Rev. ed. New York: Norton, 1980.

Heinrich, Bernd. *Mind of the Raven.* New York: Harper-Collins, 1999.

Heinz Center. *The State of the Nation's Ecosystems.* New York: Cambridge University Press, 2002.

Heschel, Abraham. *The Prophets: An Introduction.* New York: Harper Torchbooks, 1969.

Hill, Steven. *Fixing Elections: The Failure of America's Winner Take All Politics.* London: Routledge, 2002.

Holdren, John. "Energy: Asking the Wrong Question." *Scientific American,* January 2002, 65–67.

Homer-Dixon, Thomas. *The Ingenuity Gap.* New York: Knopf, 2000.

Johnson, Chalmers. *The Sorrows of Empire.* New York: Metropolitan Books, 2004.

Jones, Howard Mumford. *The Age of Energy.* New York: Viking Press, 1971.

Kammen, Michael. *A Machine That Would Go of Itself.* New York: Knopf, 1987.

Kaplan, Robert. "Was Democracy Just a Moment?" *The Atlantic Monthly,* December 1997, 55–80.

Kelly, Marjorie. *The Divine Right of Capital.* San Francisco: Barrett-Koehler, 2001.

Kelman, Steven. "Why Public Ideas Matter." In *The Power of Public Ideas,* edited by Robert Reich. Cambridge, MA: Harvard University Press, 1988.

Kennedy, Robert F. *Crimes Against Nature.* New York: HarperCollins, 2004.

Kerr, Richard. "Climate Modelers See Scorching Future as a Real Possibility." Science 307 (January 28, 2005): 497.

Kirby, Terry. "Global Warming Kills 150,000 a Year, Warns UN." *Independent* (UK), December 12, 2003.

Klare, Michael. *Blood and Oil.* New York: Metropolitan Books, 2004.

Lapham, Lewis. "Tentacles of Rage." *Harper's Magazine,* September 2004, 31–41.

Latour, Bruno. *We Have Never Been Modern.* Translated by Catherine Porter. Cambridge, MA: Harvard University Press, 1993.

Lazare, Daniel. *America's Undeclared War.* New York: Harcourt, 2001.

Leakey, Richard, and Roger Lewin. *The Sixth Extinction.* New York: Doubleday, 1995.

Lear, Linda. *Rachel Carson: Witness for Nature.* New York: Henry Holt, 1997.

Ledewitz, Bruce. "Establishing a Federal Constitutional Right to a Healthy Environment in Us and in Our Posterity." *Mississippi Law Journal* 68, no. 2 (1998).

———. "The Constitution of Sustainable Capitalism and Beyond." *Boston College Environmental Affairs Law Review* 29, no. 2 (2002): 229–279.

Lee, Jennifer. "A Call for Softer, Greener Language." *New York Times,* March 2, 2003.

Leopold, Aldo. *A Sand County Almanac.* New York: Oxford University Press, 1949.

Levy, Leonard. *Origins of the Bill of Rights.* New Haven: Yale University Press, 1999.

Lieven, Anatol. "The Push for War." *London Review of Books,* October 3, 2002.

Lind, Michael. *Made in Texas: George W. Bush and the Southern Makeover of American Politics.* New York: Basic Books, 2003.

Linklater, Andro. *Measuring America.* New York: Walker, 2002.

Lomborg, Bjorn. *The Skeptical Environmentalist.* New York: Cambridge University Press, 2001.

Lovejoy, Thomas. "Biodiversity: Dismissing Scientific Process." *Scientific American,* January 2002, 69–71.

Lovins, Amory, and L. Hunter Lovins. *Brittle Power.* Andover: Brick House, 1981.

Lovins, Amory, et al. *Small Is Profitable.* Old Snowmass, CO: Rocky Mountain Institute, 2002.

———. *Winning the Oil Endgame.* Old Snowmass, CO: Rocky Mountain Institute, 2004. Intro note 11.

Mahlman, Jerry. "Global Warming: Misuse of Data and Ignorance of Science." Union of Concerned Scientists. http://www.ucsusa.org.

Margulis, Lynn. *The Symbiotic Planet.* London: Phoenix, 1998.

Matthews, Richard. *If Men Were Angels.* Lawrence: University of Kansas Press, 1995.

McKibben, Bill. *Enough.* New York: Times Books, 2003.

McNeill, J. R. *Something New Under the Sun.* New York: Norton, 2000.

Meadows, Donella. "Economic Laws Clash with Planet's." *Earthlight,* (spring 2001).

———. "Places to Intervene in a System. *Whole Earth,*" (winter 1997).

Meine, Curt. *Conservation and the Progressive Movement.* Unpublished manuscript, 2002.

Menand, Louis. "Permanent Fatal Errors." *New Yorker,* December 6, 2004, 54–60.

Moravic, Hans. *Mind Children.* Cambridge, MA: Harvard University Press, 1988.

Moyers, Bill. "Welcome to Doomsday." *New York Review,* March 24, 2005, 8–10.

Myers, Norman. *Perverse Subsidies.* Washington, DC: Island Press, 2001.

Mumford, Lewis. *Technics and Civilization.* New York: Harcourt, Brace, and World, 1934.

Nace, Ted. *Gangs of America: The Rise of Corporate Power and the Disabling of Democracy.* San Francisco: Berrett-Koehler, 2003.

National Endowment for the Arts (NEA). *Reading at Risk.* Research Division Report #46. Washington, DC: NEA, 2004.

Odum, Howard T., and Elisabeth C. Odum. *A Prosperous Way Down.* Boulder: University Press of Colorado, 2001.

Ophuls, William, and Stephen Boyan. *Ecology and the Politics of Scarcity Revisited.* New York: W. H. Freeman, 1992.

Orwell, George. *A Collection of Essays.* New York: Harcourt, Brace, Jovanovich, 1981.

Piners, Walter, "British Intelligence Warned of Iraq War." *Washington Post,* May 2005.

Porter, Theodore. *Trust in Numbers.* Princeton: Princeton University Press, 1995.

Price, Colin. *Time, Discounting, and Value.* London: Routledge, 1993.

Raffensperger, Carolyn, and Joel Tickner, eds. *Protecting Public Health and the Environment.* Washington, DC: Island Press, 1999.

Ricketts, Taylor, et al. *Terrestrial Ecoregions of North America: A Conservation Assessment.* Washington, DC: Island Press, 1999.

Ridley, Matt. "The Profits of Doom." *The Spectator,* February 23, 2002, 10–11.

Rosenthal, Elizabeth. "Study Puts Iraqi Deaths of Civilians at 100,000." *New York Times,* October 29, 2004.

Schell, Jonathan. *The Unconquerable World.* New York: Metropolitan Books, 2003.

Scherer, Glenn. "The Godly Must Be Crazy," *Grist Magazine,* October 27, 2004. http://www.grist.org/news/maindish/2004/10/27/scherer-christian.

Schneider, Stephen. "Global Warming: Neglecting the Complexities." *Scientific American,* January 2002, 62–65.

Schumacher, E. F. *A Guide for the Perplexed.* New York: Harper and Row, 1977.

Scott, James C. *Seeing like a State.* New Haven: Yale University Press, 1998.

Simon, Jonathan, and Ron Baiman. "The 2004 Presidential Election." Unpublished paper, December 28, 2004.

Smil, Vaclav. *Energy at the Crossroads.* Cambridge: MIT Press, 2003.

Smith, Lillian. *Killers of the Dream.* New York: Norton, 1978.

Stone, Christopher. *Should Trees Have Standing?* Los Altos, CA: William Kaufman, 1974.

Stringfellow, William. *An Ethic for Christians and Other Aliens in a Strange Land.* Waco, TX: Word Books, 1973.

Sunstein, Cass. *The Second Bill of Rights.* New York: Basic Books, 2004.

———. *Designing Democracy.* New York: Oxford University Press, 2001.

———. *The Partial Constitution.* Cambridge, MA: Harvard University Press, 1993.

Suskind, Ron. *The Price of Loyalty.* New York: Simon and Schuster, 2004.

Tainter, Joseph. *The Collapse of Complex Societies.* Cambridge: Cambridge University Press, 1988.

Tannen, Deborah. "Let Them Eat Words." *American Prospect*, September 2003, 29–31.

Thornton, Joe. *Pandora's Poison.* Cambridge, MA: MIT Press, 2000.

Toulmin, Stephen. *Cosmopolis.* Chicago: University of Chicago Press, 1990.

———. *Return to Reason.* Cambridge, MA: Harvard University Press, 2001.

Tucker, Mary E. *Worldly Wonder.* Chicago: Open Court, 2003.

Turner, Jack. *The Abstract Wild.* Tucson: University of Arizona Press, 1996.

U.S. Geological Survey. *Status and Trends of the Nation's Biological Resources.* 2 vols. Washington, DC: U.S. Government Printing Office, 1998.

Vig, Norman, and Michael Kraft, eds. *Environmental Policy,* 4th ed. Washington, DC: Congressional Quarterly Press, 2000.

Walkom, Thomas. "Return of the Old, Cold War." *Toronto Star,* September 28, 2002.

Wallis, Jim. *God's Politics.* New York: Harper, 2005.

Webb, Walter Prescott.*The Great Frontier.* Austin: University of Texas Press, 1951/1975.

Wilson, E. O. *Biophilia.* Cambridge, MA: Harvard University Press, 1984.

———. *The Diversity of Life.* Cambridge, MA: Harvard University Press, 1992.

———. *The Future of Life.* New York: Knopf, 2002.

Wise, Steven. *Rattling the Cage.* Cambridge, MA: Perseus Books, 2000.

Wolin, Sheldon, *Politics and Vision.* Princeton: Princeton University Press, 2004.

Woodward, Bob. *Bush at War.* New York: Simon and Schuster, 2003.

World Commission on Environment and Development (Brundtland Commission). *Our Common Future.* New York: Oxford University Press, 1987.

Zakaria, Fareed. *The Future of Freedom.* New York: Norton, 2003.